SELF-WORTH IN CHILDREN AND YOUNG PEOPLE

SELF-WORTH IN CHILDREN AND YOUNG PEOPLE

CRITICAL AND PRACTICAL CONSIDERATIONS

Rachel Burr

Routledge
Taylor & Francis Group

LONDON AND NEW YORK

First published in 2022 by Critical Publishing Ltd

Published 2025 by Routledge
4 Park Square, Milton Park, Abingdon, Oxon OX14 4RN
605 Third Avenue, New York, NY 10017

Routledge is an imprint of the Taylor & Francis Group,
an informa business

British Library Cataloguing in Publication Data
A CIP record for this book is available from the British Library

ISBN: 9781914171772 (pbk)
ISBN: 9781041056843 (ebk)

Cover and text design by Out of House Limited

DOI: 10.4324/9781041056843

Contents

About the author

Rachel Burr

Rachel Burr is a senior lecturer in the School of Education and Social Work at the University of Sussex, where she was instrumental in establishing postgraduate and undergraduate programmes in Childhood and Youth Studies. Until recently she was course lead on the BA in Childhood and Youth. Rachel also teaches on qualifying programmes in social work. An anthropologist and social worker with an international background in child protection, her overarching focus is on developing practitioner-orientated techniques for working with and enhancing emotional strength among children and young people who are living in challenging and difficult circumstances.

For Steve, my kind and brilliant husband,

'We walked the bostall and in doing so found each other'

and

For Conrad, Charlie and Joseph, the three boy kings, now such wonderfully good men.

I love all four of you so very much.

Acknowledgements

My grateful thanks go to all the children and young people I have worked with as a social worker and researcher, and especially to those who so willingly took part in the group work that informs this book.

Colleagues at the University of Sussex have created a stimulating working environment. I particularly appreciate the ideas generated by Michelle Lefevre, Liam Berriman, Rachel Thomson, Kristi Hickle, Robert James, Reima Anna Maglajlic, Gillian Hampden Thomson, Rebecca Stephens, Simon Thompson, James and Joan Williams, Lel Meleyal, David Orr and Gillian Ruch (who also generously read some of my chapters during the editing process). When I was a doctoral student I came across Erica Burman's work within the field of child psychology, wrote to her and have continued to share ideas with her ever since. I owe a great deal to my editors Di Page and Peter Hooper. Peter never let up in his encouragement, and it is absolutely down to him that this book has been published

Writing a book of this nature inevitably takes time and over the years particular friends and family members have provided encouragement and support. My mum, Pam, spent much of her career working as a teacher and we spent many a day sharing creative approaches for bringing out the best in children. I miss her very much and her gentle approach to life continues to influence my thinking. My mum's sisters Heather and Jill continually root for me, as do Ade, Carole (or Carolyn) and Gordon. My dad, Mike, has proofread and edited and has been generous in taking the time to look over my work. My brother Simon and sister-in-law EJ are ever supportive.

Kristin has continued to share her thoughtful insights on the subject of childhood, while my friend from my teens Jon is always interested in what I'm up to. I share my love for Vietnam with my dear 'sisters' Emma, and wise Gill, and Alison and Melissa. My dear walking companion and friend Yvonne has contributed much to my thinking. Vinita is always so thoughtful and encouraging. Joanna very generously read drafts of this book. Her regular phone chats bring me such joy (there will always be a place for Red). Emily has walked along many a path with me. Ruth and Liz have also generously carved out time to join me on walks. I really enjoy being in the gentle presence of Susan. Jacqui is a very good and kind friend. Elaine, Annie and Vicky have been there and offering support throughout. The three Janes have inspired me to keep on running. And I grew up alongside two great friends Andy King and Sarah (Smithy) and hold our childhood memories close to my heart.

Finally, my lovely gentle husband, Steve, and dear sons Conrad, Charlie and Joseph have patiently listened to me talk through the themes that run through this book. They give me reason to 'always look on the bright side of life' and to live by our family lore dating back to the Normans that 'we are not in this world for ourselves alone'.

Preface

This book is useful for anyone who has an interest in mental health and who would like to positively enhance how children and young people feel about themselves and their place in the world. It introduces easily replicable, creative and supportive age-appropriate methods to support the development of resilience and a capacity to engage with and think about mental health in restorative and creative ways. The themes and methods that I introduce are designed for use with any child and young person growing up in the UK and not just those who are already receiving specialist support. All of the methods can be introduced to individuals or to groups of children, although I prefer group work, and the techniques can be shared in any setting where children and young people come together, perhaps in a school, an out-of-school club or a youth setting. I also place an emphasis on the methods being introduced in such a way that older children are encouraged to feel in control of their practice and in the long term feel confident to practise the relaxation techniques on their own.

I use the term young person rather than teenager throughout this book because some of my work has been with young people into their mid-twenties.

Background

The seeds for this book were sown during my childhood and reinforced over 25 years ago when I was in my twenties working as a hospital social worker in London, and then a child protection social worker in Dublin, Ireland. I learnt so much during that time about the complex nature of love and the loyalty of children to family members. The children and young people I worked with were often aware of both the strengths and shortcomings of the people who were raising them, and in order to survive were forced to become quite resourceful and independent minded. This meant that it took time for us to develop trusting relationships.

As is still the case today, my involvement, and that of other professionals, was really quite limited. Most children spent the majority of their time with their families going about their lives, and I often found myself worrying about the things that I couldn't control, such as how they might be treated in the aftermath of one of my visits, or whether they were at heightened risk of being hurt in some way when trusted adults were not close to hand.

In other words, I began to feel that it was impossible for me to do anything but fail the children I most wanted to protect. There are multiple reasons for this, but one key influence that I would like to highlight, and which is key to the writing of this book, relates to the very adult-centric interactions that we have with children and young people within our education and child protection systems. We rarely incorporate opportunities for children and young people to develop resilience-based coping strategies that they can be encouraged to independently draw upon at times of need. Yet, as case examples throughout this book show, children and young people positively thrive when we treat them respectfully and show that we have faith in their capacity for self-determination.

A wider context

Later I moved to Hanoi, Vietnam, where I worked with children who lived and worked on the streets or who had been locked up in government-run detention centres. I discovered that some of them were just as independent and resourceful as young people I had worked with in Ireland and London, the difference being that the Vietnamese children I knew did not live with family members and often drew strength from one another within informally created peer support networks.

Undoubtedly, a number of the children and young people I encountered in Vietnam, London and Dublin experienced unnecessary hardships and were traumatised, and sometimes sad, angry and scared. But they were also survivors who did not want to be treated as passive victims, nor did they want to be rescued and removed from their homes or the streets by concerned adults. In fact, most of the children I met heavily resisted such interventions and only became open to change when they felt that the people who were offering support had their best interests at heart.

During this time, I began to appreciate that if I wanted to be of any meaningful help then, wherever possible, I should aim to work at a child or young person's pace, and also be respectful of and recognise the techniques that each of them had developed in order to go about their daily lives and survive thus far. Experiences such as these have made me wary of adult-led intervention programmes that fail to properly consider the perspective of the children and young people they are aimed at or the remarkable strength that some individuals exhibit while managing very challenging situations.

In some ways my impetus for writing this book is a personal one. My father experienced poverty and homelessness as a child, and while I was growing up often talked about the impact that this had on him. On one occasion he recalled, he was about seven years old, living in a small caravan on a farm, and slowly counting on repeat the rain drops as they slid down the window. He was cold and hungry, and as his fingers traced the droplets, he came to the decision that it was down to him to improve his chances in life. At that tender age he resolved to work incredibly hard and take every opportunity going. And he did just that. He went on to meet my mum in his teens and continued to thrive as a result of her very grounding love. Yet even as a young child I picked up on his residual feeling of doubt in his achievements, and over time it became clear to me that without sensitive emotional support it is very hard to completely relinquish the feeling of powerlessness that comes with growing up in an unpredictable environment. I decided to become a social worker in the hope that I might be able to help a child make sense of their experiences while they were happening to them, and not as a victim, but from a position of strength. No one should be negatively influenced by aspects of their life that they are powerless to change.

Our experiences in childhood shape us, and it is therefore imperative that we work alongside individuals in support of their developing self-worth and resilience. We can only do so by directly involving them in the process and creating opportunities for individuals to contextualise and understand their experiences more fully.

A child-centred programme: the fieldwork process

Over the following years, I had children of my own, and witnessed one of my sons become more comfortable in himself when using meditative techniques. By this time, I was also working at the University of Sussex and coming across inter-disciplinary research indicating the physiological and psychological benefits of taking part in relaxation techniques, some of which were similar to those I had practised with children in Vietnam. I resolved to work directly with young people in the UK to see if we could create a programme that they could adapt and use independently at any point when they felt the need to do so.

The book layout and key themes

Every chapter in this book draws upon case study examples from my practice as a researcher, social worker and teacher; however, some chapters have a more academic focus, while others place a greater emphasis on putting methods into practice. Chapter 1 provides an introductory overview and outlines theories and ideas that have contributed to my work, particularly in relation to the current treatment of childhood within fields as diverse as child rights, child development, psychology and neuroscience. Chapter 2 examines the influence of child psychology and development, attachment theory and trauma-based approaches. It also looks at emerging influences within the fields of positive psychology and neurology. Chapter 3 looks specifically at current approaches within mental health care and discusses the diagnostic treatment of children and young people. Chapters 4, 5 and 6 focus on case study examples, fieldwork findings and the intervention programmes that young people and I developed in collaboration with each other. Chapter 7 provides additional examples of good practice for a wider range of professionals who have direct contact with children and young people, while Chapter 8 presents concluding comments drawn from each chapter.

Working with young children

Most of the approaches outlined in Chapter 4 focus on young children, and are methods that I picked up as a social worker as a result of my research interests. Because of the emphasis on body safety, techniques outlined for younger children need to be more adult directed, and if you work in early-year or school settings it would be advisable to ask for parental approval before introducing some of the themes that we cover.

Working with older children and young people

The core practices for older children outlined in this book were designed in collaboration with a group of secondary school students. I worked with them as a researcher over a five-year period to see if it was possible to develop a support programme that young people would want to go on to practise independently in privately chosen moments during any given day.

The students and I homed in on what worked well. Time and time again I found that individuals felt happiest moving through the relaxation and meditative practices, and following the same sequences week on week.

With this last point in mind, do take time to familiarise yourself with the exercises, remembering that each child or young person will need to do the same in order to make their practice meaningful to them. The techniques we developed only work because they have been created alongside, and in conjunction with, other exploratory practices that have provided individuals with time to explore the themes and life experiences which they chose to bring to our sessions.

Added benefits

The methods introduced to you in this book are intended to create a healthy environment in which it is possible for all children and young people to participate, get to know each other and learn to respectfully support their peers in small group settings. This type of group work can help individuals to feel less isolated, and create an environment in which people can safely begin to recognise that they are not alone in sometimes feeling emotions such as sadness, worry and fear, and also happiness, contentment and satisfaction from caring for others. Working in this way has had the added bonus of supporting the development of good interpersonal skills, which can also in turn support young people towards feeling greater self-confidence.

Finally, it is possible to dip into this book and focus primarily on chapters that have a practical element to them, but if you have the space and time then I would encourage you to read the chapters in the order that I wrote them. The ideas that I advocate are informed by a wide range of theories and disciplines and provide necessary context for our practice.

Rachel

1 An introduction

To give us back to ourselves—there lies the great, the singular power of self-respect. Without it, one eventually discovers the final turn of the screw: one runs away to find oneself and finds no one at home.

Joan Didion (1968)

This book outlines new ways to understand and support children and young people's emotional well-being. It introduces easily replicated approaches and techniques that anyone qualified to work with children and young people in any type of child or youth-focused setting can use. It also examines current ideas about young people's mental health and highlights an urgent need for us to treat children and teenagers with greater understanding and respect.

As a society we tend to infantilise and marginalise young people, and we are also not very good at listening to or encouraging children to develop healthy relationships with their emotions. Yet, as my work demonstrates, it is possible to provide even very young children with the skills and resources to feel more in control of their lives so that they become better prepared to enhance and develop their *own* resilience and sense of self. Positive improvements in this area can be achieved, as the following chapters show, by working with children and teenagers in small group settings using child-led, person-centred and strength-based approaches that draw upon their capacity to develop self-care and in some cases offer mutual support to each other.

In short, this book outlines methods for working with children and teenagers that take the focus away from a standardised approach of working just with the individual. Instead, these methods take into consideration broader influences in each person's life and wider societal stress factors that contribute to sometimes making children feel powerless and unhappy. By taking this broader structural perspective it immediately becomes evident that there is still far more that we can do as a society if we sincerely wish to offer our children the quality of mental health support that they deserve. The good news is that a number of the ideas outlined in this book are very easy to implement. The more challenging news is that some of the practices I refer to in these pages, which are taken from my direct work and research with children, raise serious questions about our general treatment of children, and particularly teenagers.

A starting point

So, let's start at the beginning. As I write this book, I count myself as incredibly fortunate to work in an engaging and stimulating environment, surrounded by colleagues who have a passion for what they do, and by students who want to learn and are happy to critically respond to ideas generated in class by sharing their responses, thoughts and perspectives. As a result, I have been able to learn a great deal from the people around me, and particularly from the undergraduates who make up the majority of my classes. I have also learnt a great deal as a social worker and as a student adviser supporting young people's academic and emotional needs as they navigate the transition to adult independence.

In some of our teaching sessions my students and I practise the same techniques outlined in later chapters of this book. We also compare and contrast our childhood experiences and consider societal attitudes towards mental health and well-being. What it means to be well and to have good mental health is open to wide interpretation. I have opted, for reasons that will become clearer in later chapters, to use Martin Seligman's definition of well-being, which he suggests consists of having *positive emotions*, being *engaged* in an activity, having good *relationships* with other people, finding *meaning* in one's life and a sense of *accomplishment* in the pursuit of one's goals (Seligman, 2011).

Our class discussions lean towards Seligman's understanding of well-being and are also informed by subjects as diverse as the history of childhood, child development, mental health, anthropology, social policy, social work practice, law and education. Taking such influences into consideration, it becomes evident that childhood does not incorporate a fixed set of experiences. In other words, children's lives are shaped by the family and society in which they are raised, and by their and their carers' level of engagement with the dominant issues of the day.

The subject areas I cover also show that our cultural understanding of childhood, children and youth is rife with contradictions and tensions. Take, for example, our heightened focus on age as a measure of ability, where it is sometimes important to connect ability and age, but at other times chronological age may be considered more important than competence (Forster, 2010). In some contexts, we distinguish between separate stages of childhood, starting with babyhood and early infancy, and treat children as if they are not quite whole or autonomous self-determined individuals. The anthropologist Charlotte Hardman (2001) likens this tendency to children and young people having their voices muted. Yet at the international level, under the globally recognised auspices of an international human rights framework and the United Nations Convention on the Rights of the Child (UNCRC) (1989), we refer to childhood on the global stage as a homogenous rights-based experience, in which children of all ages should be treated as having capacity to understand their participatory rights regardless of their immediate circumstances. Because international laws are not legally binding but only obligatory, the response to participatory rights has been inconsistent. Hence not all countries have chosen to incorporate aspects of the UNCRC into their national laws. In 2004, the UK government ratified a Children Act, which emphasises an expectation on all of us to value and properly work with children and young people and to encourage their participation in relation to key life decisions; in other words, their views and wishes should be taken into account. However, as Burman (2007), Boyden et al (2015), Montgomery (2008), Kilkelly and Lundy (2017), Wyness (2019) and others have shown, our relationship with children is complicated by an adult need to protect.

The tension between a protectionist model and a rights-based directive to give children and young people more automony creates confusion for all concerned. In some cases children may be encouraged to have opinions, only for them to later come to the realisation that their viewpoint actually counts for little. I wonder if the rise in reported mental health issues among our young could be linked to the contradictory way in which they are treated.

A mental health crisis among our young people?

I have a growing number of students year on year who come to me to talk about themselves in relation to their mental health, and who link their experiences of distress to particular conditions, including anxiety, depression, issues relating to their identity, the challenges they face because of neurodiversity, and the difficulties that they have with engaging with other students because they feel unable to attend class. On the face of it we are making great strides towards 'acknowledging' and 'diagnosing' expressions of unhappiness and worry during childhood, and we now have diagnostic terminology for referencing our feelings. I feel concerned, however, by the current shift taking place for *some* young people growing up in the UK today. The capacity to express emotions should surely only be treated as a starting point, with the development of coping strategies and theraputic interventions to follow, rather than an end goal? Over time, I have become interested in the influences shaping such ideas and the extent to which cultural practices contribute to our expectations of children and particularly teenagers. As Prout (2005) and McLaughin et al (2016) have pointed out, childhood is not a natural state but is filled with content by its contemporary environments.

The cultural construction of adolescence

Stereotypical ideas about teenagers and adolescence often link the adolescent life stage to rebellious and sometimes disruptive behaviour. Prejudice, particularly against boys from lower socio-economic strata, is well documented. But if we wrongly assume that all teenagers will exhibit challenging behaviour, then it can also become hard to distinguish between fleeting upsets and complex forms of distress.

The man who decided that being a teenager is a struggle

In 1904, the developmental psychologist G Stanley Hall coined the term *adolescence* as a stage when a person was no longer a child, but not as yet an adult. His work and ideas about this new life stage have permeated our understanding of youth. In addition, our associations with being a teenager in the West are also linked to individualism and the tensions that arise between young people and their parents during the stage when young people are moving towards greater independence. In the UK, as in most post-industrial societies, the teenage years are stereotypically associated with contradictory experiences, rebellion and experimentation. Having a secure family base obviously makes a huge difference to young people's coping strategies, as does having good friends and being part of a positive and supportive environment in school. Yet as a result of Hall's work we tend to put emphasis on this stage in life as one being one that is particularly unsettled and transitory.

Today's young people

I have worked with children and young people for over 25 years, and what I am witnessing now, in terms of how the young people I work with talk about and understand themselves, marks a departure from the ways that they previously expressed themselves. It is witnessing this shift in how young people are presenting themselves to me in higher education, juxtaposed against the very positive shifts that I witnessed secondary school children making while on the supportive programme we developed together, that prompted me to write this book.

We have failed some young people (but we can change this)

Quite a lot of my undergraduate students come to me to tell me that they have a mental health issue that has not been formally assessed but they have self-diagnosed. There is an added tendency for the young people I meet to think of their mental health condition as fixed and permanent. In other words, they do not believe that the feelings they are experiencing will pass. They also do not always have a clear sense of where they should go for support and some of them actively avoid going to their GP for guidance.

In general, the language they use is also altering so that they no longer refer to themselves as sad, or worried or upset, but instead describe themselves as feeling anxious, traumatised and depressed. In other words, it is becoming normal for children and teenagers to refer directly to their mental health quite candidly. It is also becoming quite standard for their carers and parents to do so. While there is every reason to applaud our new openness and capacity for expressing ourselves, by the same token there is surely some need for caution. We need to step back from the experiences of the individual and ask larger questions about how we got here. Why it is that so many people seem to be unhappy? Why is it that they refer to the quality of their mental health in such disempowered and generalised terms?

I do not claim to have all the answers, far from it, but I have put together some of my observations, which take us away from thinking just about the way that young people now talk about their mental health. Instead, we should think more broadly about the possibility that inter-related influences are contributing to young people's perception that their mental health is in decline. For example, might it be that contemporary childhood is not providing enough opportunities for children to act under their own initiative and hence learn skills that could lead to greater independence and resilience? The reasons for these changes are no doubt multi-faceted, so what follows is an outline of *possible* contributory factors.

The changing face of childhood

Childhood freedoms have changed. As recently as the 1990s, children and teenagers had far more physical freedom. They walked to school from a very young age by themselves, made camps in woods, hung out on the streets outside their homes and were able to roam free. Most children growing up today do not experience such freedoms. As a society we are more risk-averse than we have ever been. Childhood and the job of growing up has now flipped on its head, and children's worlds have generally shrunk into the private domain of the home and the institutional setting of schools. Peter Gray (2011) points out that since the 1960s in the United States and other developing countries, children's free play with other children has declined sharply; his findings suggest that decline in play has contributed to the rise in psychopathology because play functions as a means to learn to get on with people, feel joy and regulate feelings.

Today's children have very limited options for the creation of personal space away from their adult minders. It is perhaps partly because of this that the online world now holds such huge and widespread appeal because it is online that children find their freedoms. Where once in the not-too-distant past they would have done so down alleys, in parks and on the streets while hanging out unsupervised among their friends, now their most immediate option is to retreat into their bedrooms and on to their mobile phone or gaming devices. In short, within the physical realm childhood has become a very well-guarded and protected space, while in the online world the opposite is the case. Where internet blockers are not in place, their interactions continue to go unregulated and tied into carefully designed social media platforms or general online content fed by algorithms that reinforce content in a highly addictive manner.

The internet

Nothing of what I am writing is new. We know what is happening to our children; we just seem to be almost powerless to act on our concerns. There are class divides at play here. Those children being raised in more affluent homes are more likely to spend their spare time taking part in out-of-school clubs and activities (all of which are adult led). This also means that regardless of opportunity, down time no longer provides children or teenagers with easy relief and respite from the outside world. It is very difficult to properly retreat and have good-quality downtime if a phone is pinging, notifications are flashing up, our friends are online and gaming, or our social media messages are in overdrive. It is easy to sound out of touch with the modern world when raising some of these issues. There are fantastic advantages to having access to the internet, and being able to walk around with a mobile phone to hand can make life so much easier but, as I show in later chapters, the online world is all consuming for some young people I work with.

Ill-thought-through solutions

A dominant approach currently adopted to try to improve our children's lives (and by this, I mean ALL of our children, not just those within our own families) focuses on introducing reductionist and siloed solutions to complex problems. As one example, asking our children to manage and learn how to healthily enjoy their time online will only work if we also actively do something to replace their online time with something that is meaningful to them.

Fear of the outside world

We tend not to let our children out of our sight because we are scared that they will be run over or abducted. While we might know such fears to be statistically very unlikely to happen to a child, bad things do happen to some children (ironically most often within the private domain of the home). Yet we have a media that fuels the fear of the stranger. We are also surrounded by other parents who, like us, are fearful and will also not allow their children out. So, to do so is to do something quite extraordinary. It is very difficult to buck the expectation that children should be with an adult without feeling like an inadequate and somewhat naïve child-caring professional or parent. It is understandable, then, that few people are going to run the risk of giving children more physical freedoms until other members of their community do likewise. Packs of children roaming free (as some of us experienced growing up) make for a strong unit. The lone child, we rationalise, is easy prey.

The fact that we pretty much all know this makes the knowledge that we are doing very little to challenge the status quo or have a nationally led discussion about how to create more freedoms for our children all the more depressing.

So why aren't we thinking in wider societal terms? Other societies are not safeguarding children quite in the way that we do. In fact, our approach is out of sync with that of many other countries. In Norway, Denmark and Sweden it is commonplace for children to walk to school by themselves from as young as six years old, likewise in Japan and Switzerland where children are actively expected to walk to school independently in order to learn self-reliance and build healthy resilience. In fact, in 2017 the European Union published a recommendation that all children would benefit from going backwards and forwards to school by themselves during primary years (Noack, 2016).

The changing face of education

Until recently, school was the place that students attended in order to receive an information and curriculum-informed education. There was neither the scope nor space for students to formally express their feelings and emotions. Teachers taught, and supported or reprimanded if children acted out. Unhappy and disruptive pupils were far more likely to be given a detention or the cane than to receive child-centred and empathic support. Yet this did not mean that childhood distress went unnoticed. Thanks to informal networks and pupil-led communication channels, I recall being aware of who among us had more complicated lives. From a young age, my friends and I were aware that a boy in our year called James was in foster care, that a girl called Judy had a mother who was unable to care for her, and that Sophie's father was most likely abusing her. As we moved up through the school years, I could also see that Sophie was purposely choosing not to wash and to look dishevelled in the heartbreaking hope that being unkempt would result in her father leaving her alone. I sensed the sadness in some of these experiences but did not have the words to hand to discuss what I was observing or know which adult in the school could be trusted to appropriately intervene. The problem remained that we had neither the knowledge nor the language to act on our concerns. It was a sad time for children and young people who did not feel like they quite fitted the mould, or who had been let down by the adults in their life and were being mistreated.

Some positives

Moving swiftly on, and fast-tracking forward to the landscape of contemporary childhood, I would argue that an enormous amount has changed – in general for the better. Today we are more open about our feelings, and we are moving towards becoming a society in which the different forms of child abuse can be age-appropriately discussed. In fact, if you need further support on this topic there are plenty of examples of how to introduce protective language to young children in this book.

We now recognise that poor treatment has an effect on our mental health and well-being. On that basis, it could be argued that we are living in more liberating and safer times. However, now might be the time to reflect on how far we have come and celebrate, but also to reflect on how much more we still need to do if we want young people to think about their mental health in a positive manner.

The UK as a quick-fix society

Somewhere along the way, during our transition from being a nation in which it was standard practice to bury and repress difficult experiences towards being one in which reference to mental difficulties and well-being has become culturally acceptable, we seem to have lost sight of what constitutes a normal range of emotions. I am far from alone in thinking that this might be the case. During the process of writing this book, I have spoken to a wide range of professionals, including medics, counsellors and student support workers, all of whom are experiencing a rise in individuals turning to professionals when they are experiencing low-level experiences of distress. As a result, it is becoming harder to distinguish between urgent and low-level mental health needs and support services for young people who may feel that they are at crisis point.

This lack of balance in how we engage with our emotions also reflects the contradictory way we refer to mental health; either as a medical and diagnosable condition linked to taking prescription-based drugs or sometimes as something that is fixable via our engagement with guided practice in well-being and mindfulness. It is almost as if we have entered a realm where we are either meant to be happy (our children are under all sorts of pressure to fulfil a romantic representation of innocence and care-free existence), or, if we are feeling low, meant to act as if the experience is an extreme one. Yet there are a multitude of ways of thinking about and addressing mental health, most of which would be challenging to adequately address using only these approaches.

The changing definition of childhood

Our shift towards extending childhood has been a gradual one and can be understood in relation to a wide range of influences, including family size, qualification-linked workplace opportunities and education laws. For example, since 2015 all young people growing up in the UK have been required to be in some form of part-time education or skilled training until they turn 18. The resulting shift away from paid work towards an emphasis on education has seen some positive changes and a general rise in qualification levels across the population. However, it has also resulted in young people having to stay financially dependent on their immediate family for longer than they would have done in the past, and while for the majority this probably does not prove too much of a problem, for some this is far from ideal and can be difficult to manage. It might also be that our extension of childhood within the education system also affects how children and young people are understood in terms of their level of competence more generally.

We are generally quite good at supporting younger children, but teenagers are often given quite bad press; there is a widely held societal assumption that adolescence is a challenging time and a period of rebellion. As a society I think we do a great disservice to our young. Stereotypes aside, most young people do pretty well while managing the narrow range of options that we make available to them during this period in their lives. From the age of 11 onwards, our young people enter a stage of life that is more driven by exams and testing than ever before. This, coupled with our acceptance that the teenage years are going to be challenging, almost creates a perfect storm of high anxiety and depression. We both infantilise and limit earning opportunities for teenagers and impose a form of testing on them that only suits particular personality types.

Jumping from point A to Z without pause

On the face of it, we are making great strides towards 'acknowledging', 'diagnosing' and 'fixing' expressions of unhappiness and worry during childhood, but our emphasis is still on the treatment of the lone individual. It is the child who gets a diagnosis, or in some cases the sad and worried young person who trails the internet searching for a rationale for a feeling of disconnect, who then comes up with their own explanation and a diagnosis for why it is that they feel they way they do. Individual children and teenagers then sit with a label, and in some cases a clinical diagnosis, which describes what is wrong with them, and the experience of being examined and thought of as having a condition becomes a large part of who they understand themselves to be. In essence, the whole process means that we are overly focused on the individual as being outside and separate from wider influences that undoubtedly shape their lives: the family members they are surrounded by, the friends they have, the education setting they are in, and the type of support services society has on offer to them. This makes for an isolating experience, and prevents us thinking more creatively and restoratively about some of the liberation that can be found in putting context to the pressures to which children may feel that they are being subjected.

Instead, it would be more useful to place children and young people at the centre of their own mental health journey. This book shows you how to engage with children creatively and positively while also moving away from a deficit model of mental health to properly engage them in ways that encourage the most vulnerable children, those who are least likely to give voice to their experiences.

Moving forward

As a society, we have only recently become interested in and open to talking about mental health and well-being. So as the following chapters highlight, we simply do not have adequate data to substantiate the claim that mental health problems are on the rise. And is it not depressing and fatalistic of us to draw such soul-destroying arguments anyway? We need to show children how to enjoy life, to accept that inevitably there will be difficulties along the way, and to give them the resources to learn how to ride out discomforts, disappointments and loss, and to believe in themselves.

It would be far more humane and positive to instead recognise that our newly awakened interest in mental health issues is now at a crossroads. We could choose to continue along the trajectory of focusing on medical intervention in the form of creating diagnoses and prescription-led support or we could combine this approach with a broader holistic range of empathetically devised support services. As this book should make clear, I prefer the latter route, which also happily and coincidentally mirrors the most recent National Institute for Health and Care Excellence (NICE) guidelines published in November 2021, in which group and individual therapy should be the first line of support to people experiencing mental health difficulties (Gregory, 2021; NICE, 2021). Initiatives such as these indicate positive shifts in how we think about mental health, but with that last point in mind it is easy to forget how far we have come).

Childhood is still a time of feeling powerless

Yet as the case examples referred to throughout this book demonstrate, there is still so much more to do. Adults still hold the driving seat, and we still do not always adequately listen to children or always actively respond to theirs and other people's concerns when their well-being is under threat. We have a longstanding history of treating children as immature and, by fact of their physical and cognitive development, incomplete. This means that we do not always take their views seriously. We need to listen to children, but also teach all of them collectively by introducing fun and light-hearted sessions into the school day from a young age, so that we focus on resilience and contentment rather than poor mental health.

Conclusion

When we tell people they are sick they will begin to feel unwell, and when we respond to children who are having emotional difficulties by offering a medical diagnosis, or they hear that poor mental health is on the rise, they will feel bad about themselves and their carers will feel worried for them. It is time that we re-engaged with the myriad of emotions that make us human. This book challenges the stereotypes that we fall into when thinking about childhood and youth. It raises important questions about the ways in which we are thinking about and treating mental health.

Far more importantly, it should show you that well-grounded, sensible and easily achievable approaches can be introduced to ALL children and young people. Everyone should have the chance to grow up in supportive and caring environments, so that they can become thoughtful, engaged, robust and well balanced. To do so is a form of liberation. This book outlines methods for developing life skills that look beyond the individual and support children and young people with the aim that they can begin to feel less disconnected from others. There are five clear steps that, with help, they can be encouraged to take. They can:

1. identify their own problems/possibilities;

2. have the language to speak about difficulties;

3. know that adults will listen and respond properly;

4. identify solutions/responses to these challenges;

5. take personal or collective action.

Let us now see how we can address these issues.

References

Boyden, J, Dercon, S and Abhijeet, S (2015) Child Development in a Changing World: Risks and Opportunities. *The World Bank Research Observer*, 30(2): 193–219.

Burman, E (2007) *Deconstructing Developmental Psychology*. London: Routledge.

Children Act 2004 [online] Available at: www.legislation.gov.uk/ukpga/2004/31/contents (accessed 18 June 2022).

Didion, J (1968) *Slouching Towards Bethlehem*. Sunnyvale, CA: Farrar, Straus and Giroux.

Forster, S (2010) Age-Appropriateness: Enabler or Barrier to a Good Life for People with Profound Intellectual and Multiple Disabilities? *Journal of Intellectual and Developmental Disabilities*, 35(2): 129–31.

Gray, P (2011) The Decline in Play and the Rise of Psychopathology in Children and Adolescents. *American Journal of Play*, 3(4): 443–61.

Gregory, A (2021) NHS to Give Therapy for Depression Before Medication Under New Guidelines. *The Guardian*, 22 November. [online] Available at: www.theguardian.com/society/2021/nov/23/nhs-to-give-therapy-for-depression-before-medication-under-new-guidelines (accessed 18 June 2022).

Hall, G S (1904) *Adolescence*. Stanford, CA: Stanford University Press.

Hardman, C (2001) Can There Be an Anthropology of Children? *Childhood*, 8(4): 501–17.

Kilkelly, U and Lundy, L (2017) *Children's Rights*. London: Routledge.

McLaughlin, J, Coleman-Fountain, E and Clavering, E (2016) *Disabled Childhoods. Monitoring Differences and Emerging Identities*. London: Routledge.

Montgomery, H (2008) *An Introduction to Childhood: Anthropological Perspectives on Children's Lives*. Oxford: Wiley-Blackwell.

NICE (2021) NICE Creates New Menu of Treatment Options for Those Suffering from Depression. [online] Available at: www.nice.org.uk/news/nice-creates-new-menu-of-treatment-options-for-those-suffering-from-depression (accessed 18 June 2022).

Noack, R (2016) Let 6-year-olds Walk to School Alone, European Officials Advise Parents. *Washington Post*, 4 November. [online] Available at: www.washingtonpost.com/news/worldviews/wp/2016/11/04/let-6-year-olds-walk-to-school-alone-european-officials-advise-parents/ (accessed 5 August 2022).

NSPCC (2022) Keeping Children Safe. [online] Available at: www.nspcc.org.uk/ keep ing- child ren- safe (accessed 18 June 2022).

Prout, A (2005) *The Future of Childhood*. London: Routledge.

Seligman, M (2011) *Flourish: A New Understanding of Happiness and Wellbeing: The Practical Guide to Using Positive Psychology to Make You Happier and Healthier*. Philadelphia, PA: Nicholas Brearley Publishing.

United Nations Convention on the Rights of the Child (UNCRC) (1989) [online] Available at: www.unicef.org.uk/what-we-do/un-convention-child-rights (accessed 18 June 2022).

Wyness, M (2019) *Childhood, Culture and Society: In a Global Context*. London: Macmillan.

2 Mental health, well-being and culture

If you want others to be happy, practice compassion. If you want to be happy, practice compassion.

Dalai Lama (in Dalai Lama and Cutler, 1998)

This chapter examines ways in which Western-driven developmental psychology and psychiatry have come to dominate how we think about and treat children and young people during their formative years. It refers to the most influential and relevant approaches in the field, alongside wider cultural practices that shape our dominant ideas about childhood. A central theme running through this chapter is that children in post-industrial societies are understood with reference to psychology-based developmental life-stage theories. Within this approach, the stages of childhood are mapped out so that childhood is recognised as a time of immaturity and individuals are treated as 'child-like' or incomplete until they reach the age of 18, when they legally become adults. For children growing up in loving, stimulating home and school environments, the resulting extension of childhood is unlikely to cause too many problems. But for children growing up in difficult or abusive home environments and/or going to schools that do not have the scope to properly support their learning needs, the experience of an extended childhood can feel very different.

This shift has had an effect on education policy and employment law, resulting in young people having to stay economically reliant on their elders. They can no longer leave school at 16 and are expected to stay in some form of education or voluntary work until they turn 18. This, coupled with few employment opportunities, further hinders young people's ability to live independently and to be properly heard. This extension of dependency creates an environment in which unhappy children and young people are vulnerable to further abuses of power. Few options exist for young people to proactively make self-determined change during their adolescence, and their upset, particularly when expressed as anger or social withdrawal, is often viewed unsympathetically or simply as a rite of passage to being a teenager. Some children might seem to respond well to such an approach, but as suggested throughout this book, sensitive and therapeutic-minded forms of intervention should also be incorporated whenever young people express strong emotions, whether that be as anger or withdrawal. Failure to support distressed and vulnerable young people can be deeply damaging, as the following example illustrates.

Institutional abuse

I came across the following case of institutional abuse when I was visiting and assessing the practice of one of my social work students on her social work placement at a private foster care agency. My student Rose's work involved overseeing the placement care of children looked after by the agency, and over the course of a few months she had been working with Mia, a 15-year-old girl who was living away from her home area as the only child in a two-parent foster care setting. During tutorials Rose had told me that Mia had previously experienced a very unsettled time with her biological mother, who had repeatedly thrown her out of the family home. Yet despite this history, all was going well: Mia was studying hard for her GCSEs, and was starting to develop a cautiously trusting relationship with both my student and with her foster carers. However, unknown to Mia or Rose, the foster carers had previously told the foster care agency manager that they would be happy to take a sibling group into their home should the need arise. Unexpectedly, two days before our placement meeting, a sibling group was referred to the agency. Because the agency was short on placements the manager decided, in collaboration with the foster carers, but without consulting either Rose or Mia, to replace Mia with the sibling group. Mia was not forewarned of this monumental change to her circumstances and when my student turned up to organise the move Mia, quite understandably, became very distressed, distraught and angry. Rather than de-escalate Mia's expression of fear and rejection, the foster carers further exacerbated the situation by calling the police, which resulted in Mia being given a caution.

In this case, the needs of the agency and foster carers had clearly taken precedent over anything else. When I arrived at the agency for the placement meeting, Rose was upset and worried about Mia, and during our brief one-on-one chat was able to think about Mia's reaction from an attachment and trauma-based perspective. It was not an ideal case to focus on for our meeting but, unfortunately, because it was Rose's only social work case we had no choice but to discuss it. Naively, I expected the manager to be both embarrassed and apologetic. When I reflect on our meeting, I am still concerned by the unwillingness of the foster care manager to think about the emotional distress that the unexpected termination of the placement had caused to Mia, and in particular the way that her poor handling of a potential move had mirrored exactly what Mia had experienced whenever her mother had thrown her out of the family home.

The treatment of Mia was deeply triggering for her, and was further exacerbated by the fact that Mia had been starting to lower her guard and tentatively develop a trusting relationship with her carers. In front of her foster care manager my student Rose remained mute, and meekly agreed when the manager justified her actions by stating that Mia was out of control and unplaceable. This did not bode well for Rose, who in the context of the placement felt incapable to act as an advocate for Mia and instead towed the line of the agency. Aside from sharing my concerns in the meeting, my follow-on response was to advise our placement officer to withdraw from using the placement in the future. As for Mia? Her social worker placed her elsewhere. But, like so many young people who enter the care system, Mia deserved far better, and would have been better served if the adults making decisions on her behalf had proper insight into attachment theory, trauma-induced distress and the long-term effects of growing up in chaotic family homes. In short, Mia needed the involvement of adults in her life who understand that young people's distress is not based on an innate drive to be difficult but rather is a cry for insightful care and support.

In general, contemporary engagement with children and teenagers leans towards a deficit model of care – one in which our focus is on the behaviour of individual young people and not on the organisations that sometimes fail to support them. However, there is room for optimism, and it comes in the form of combining new and emerging developments in the field of psychology with established approaches that already give insight into the psychological landscape of childhood.

(As a final caveat, psychology and child development is an extensive subject area in its own right, and there is not the scope to discuss all relevant aspects in this chapter. Wherever possible I have referenced further reading materials that might be of interest to you and I have focused on the theories that currently dominate the field of childhood studies.)

Understanding developmental psychology

As Mia's case shows, it is essential to that we have some grounding in some aspects of human growth and development. The children's author Judith Kerr notes that '*we live our lives in two distinct halves: the first half lasts until we are 18, the second is all the years that follow*' (Adams, 2021). In other words, there is little to dispute that what happens to us during our early years is hugely significant and influential in shaping how we feel about ourselves and what we expect from others.

Yet, as we learn later in this chapter, the form that this understanding takes is not universally applicable across the globe. Rather, it is shaped by a complex array of societal values and cultural influences. For example, developmental psychology compartmentalises childhood into clearly defined developmental periods such as babyhood, the early years and pre-teen years, leading on to adolescence and then adulthood at 18 years of age. These markers of childhood are routinely used by international age agencies, working with children on the basis that their life starts after birth at the age 0. This is used as a means to measure and compare normative aspects of child development in the international context and is enshrined in the United Nations Convention on the Rights of the Child (UNCRC). Yet in some parts of the world, the age of the child is not recorded and in other parts an infant is aged one at birth. I discovered this by chance while working in Vietnam among street children. For example, a child who told me he was ten was actually nine once we applied a Western framework of age measurement! Most of the aid workers I interviewed were not aware of this disparity, but it is an important one to be aware of for so many reasons, including appropriate use of immunisations, the age that a child is sent to an aid-funded school, or whether a child is fostered by a family or placed in institutional care. It means that global representations of childhood and the life-stage theories they support are not universally applicable.

Dominant influences in the field

Interest in the human psyche and child development emerged out of direct observations of children going about their daily lives, whether that be in the context of institutional settings such as orphanages or nurseries, or while children were interacting with their parents or primary carers. Our forerunners in the field of child development were inspired to study the emotional response of children because they wanted to improve the quality of their lives. Their interest and concern for children did not appear out of nowhere. The most influential child-focused psychologists drew on their experiences as members of the Jewish diaspora, a number of whom had been forced to flee Nazi persecution and resettle from Vienna to London. Significant psychoanalytic researchers in the field of child-focused psychoanalysis include Sigmund Freud's daughter Anna Freud and her rival in the field Melanie Klein.

Secure attachments in early infancy create long-term resilience

One study of particular influence is Anna Freud and Sophie Dann's war orphans study (1951), which highlights complex emotional outcomes for young children deprived of nurturing adult relationships. They worked with children aged three and over who had been rescued at the end of the Second World War from German concentration camps. Once Freud and Dann got to know each child's pre-war history, they discovered that children who had experienced secure early relationships which were then interrupted through war and trauma were able to recover and learn to build up trusting relationships if the new context was a supportive one. They also found that children who had strong and secure pre-war attachments had, when deprived of adult relationships, developed secure attachments among their peers. Judy Dunn and Carol Kendrick (1982) found similarly protective influences in their work on sibling relationships, in which strong sibling relationships can act as a mitigating factor against parental neglect and separation. They also suggest that siblings themselves have an important influence on each other's development.

The findings that emerged from these and similar studies highlight the importance of infants and children being raised in supportive and nurturing family-type small-scale settings, and have gone on to influence how we engage with children today; so much so, that many of their ideas have been incorporated into all forms of childcare practice. For example, today it is standard for any child entering an early-year setting to be paired with one member of staff. This person's role is to pay particular attention to their allocated children with the purpose of getting to know each child as an individual, so that they can sensitively respond when needed and become the child's safe and secure attachment figure in a sometimes overwhelming and noisy institutional setting.

Attachment theory

Most people with training in child development are also likely to recognise value in John Bowlby's ground-breaking work on attachment theory (1950–71), in which he coined the term 'attachment' in the 1950s to highlight the quality of the adult–infant relationship, and the long-term impact of having a secure or insecure attachment on how individuals go on to engage with their wider world. Today this theory is a mainstay of good social work practice because attachment theory is helpful for illuminating the quality of the relationship established between child and carer. As Beckett and Taylor (2019, p 53) point out, '*one way of looking at attachment is that the attachment figure is a kind of emotional anchor, a source of security*'. They also point out that the quality of our attachments is not fixed and takes a long time to develop and build up slowly during our early childhoods.

Children are powerless to influence the attachment style of their parent or carer

Attachment theory helps us appreciate that children do not have the luxury of choice when it comes to who raises them. For their very survival they have to attach to their carer and bond with them, even if their parent/carer is not managing the caring role very well. So, as one example, if a parent is inconsistent, meaning in this case that they are sometimes there for a child and sometimes not, the child will have to accommodate for this inconsistency. This will not only shape how they view their parent or general caregiver but will also create an expectation (or internal working model deep in their subconscious) that their parents' behaviour mirrors how *all* people behave (because why not? they know nothing other than their own intimate experiences).

It makes sense that children who grow up *without* an attentive and warm carer are likely to find life very difficult and disengage from others. This means that children who receive inadequate care may resort to developing their own strategies of self-soothing. Self-soothing might take the form of withdrawing into their own world as a form of protection and developing an alternative and imagined reality. For example, some children might over-eat as a form of self-comfort when they are upset and have learnt that there is no point in sharing their worries, or as they get older, they might numb their feelings of pain by using different forms of drugs and alcohol.

Strategies such as these outlined above make sense because the need to survive and thrive is a must, and with nowhere to go children will stay attached to the people who are raising them. In extreme circumstances, they may also adapt by mentally side-lining and splitting difficult and upsetting experiences off from their day-to-day thoughts and processes (this is further explained by Melanie Klein's (1923) 'object relations', a psychodynamic theory that gives insight into the way that we bury difficult and challenging experiences deep in our unconscious). In the here and now, this form of 'splitting' is very successful because it allows children to cope with sometimes unimaginably horrific experiences. A helpful example of this type of coping strategy has been described by Beth Ellis in her autobiography *Bad Things in the Night* (2010), in which she writes eloquently about a deterioration in her mental health during early adulthood. She describes having moved away from home to start university, where she began experiencing confusing and fragmented dreams involving disturbing images of herself as a young child. She initially turned to alcohol to quell the images, but they kept coming, and as a result she temporarily dropped out of university.

Over the next few years, Beth entered therapy with a highly trained specialist, and together they began to slowly piece together deeply suppressed memories of sexual abuse at the hands of her stepfather and his friends. Beth's book makes for a brave and deeply unsettling read, and yet her experiences are not uncommon. Part of her mission in writing the book was to bring criminal proceedings against her stepfather, but her case against him was dropped by the legal system. This outcome was devastating for Beth. Our legal system let her down, but wider attitudes towards childhood also contributed to her incapacity to communicate what was happening to her. It highlights a need for us to give children the language to talk about their lives and their bodies, and safe practices. School is the ideal place to do this because it is a public space in which all children can be supported alongside each other in group settings in an unthreatening way. The National Society for Prevention of Cruelty to Children (NSPCC) have developed the PANTS initiative, which includes a wide range of resources for schools to use with young children. PANTS refers to: P= Privates are Privates, A= Always remember your body belongs to you, N= No means No, T= Talk about things that upset you, and S = Speak up, someone can help. Today, Beth continues to work on this subject in her singular desire to help and support others, and to highlight the complex response that children have to cruel and destructive abuses during childhood. Perhaps if the PANTS initiative had been available when Beth was at primary school, things might have been quite different for her.

Wider values of society also shape how children and young people are treated

Other developmental theorists broadened their scope, moving away from psycho-therapeutic approaches to examine socio-cultural influences. Jean Piaget's ideas on cognitive development influence how children are schooled (1950 onwards), and the ideas developed by Eric Erikson (1968) emphasise the importance of quality in social relationships. In his work within his school of ego psychology, Erikson linked individuals' capacity to cope with day-to-day experiences with their age-linked physical and cognitive development. He suggested that individuals need to move successfully in a linear fashion from one stage to the next in order to successfully manage personal and societal expectations of them. This psycho-social theory builds on foundations laid by Sigmund Freud (1933) in acknowledging the conscious and unconscious parts of the self, while also departing from Freud in its interest in the importance of the external world as an influence on emotional and behavioural development.

Piaget's theory of cognitive development is more pertinent to an educational setting and suggests that children move through four different stages of intellectual development, reflective of the increasing sophistication of children's thoughts at each stage. He spoke of the importance of creating equilibrium, in which a child's developing understanding of the world is stable and safe. Erikson made some similar points about the importance of being raised in an interesting and supportive environment and suggested that children move through life stages in a linear fashion. He proposed that successful transition from one stage to the next is associated with safety and stimulation, both of which are needed for individuals to successfully master each stage and become productive and well-adjusted members of society. Both Piaget and Erikson's ideas highlight the importance of being raised in caring and engaging environments, and both outline the types of problems and developmental delays that can result when supportive stimulation does not occur.

No theory is without its critics

Critics have pointed out that Piaget placed too much emphasis on chronological age and underestimated the capacity for very young children to grapple with complex and conflicting ideas. For example, the sociologist Robbie Duschinsky (Duschinsky and Reijman, 2016; Duschinsky and Solomon, 2017; Duschinsky, 2020) is concerned that attachment theory has become the go-to theory for social workers. He suggests that an over-emphasis on the quality of attachments in the early years is contributing to an imbalance in where child-focused funding is directed. In general, more funding exists for children during their early years than for older children and those in their teens who would respond positively to youth-focused projects. Duschinsky also points out that both John Bowlby and his colleague Mary Ainsworth feared that attachment theory would become a bandwagon theory, and that an emphasis on attachment would become over-emphasised as a go-to theory by practitioners.

Others have found fault in Erikson's expectation that we need to move systematically from one age stage to the next if we are to develop a healthy sense of self. Nevertheless, both Piaget and Erikson recognised the ways in which our sense of self interacts with, and is shaped by, wider familial, societal and environmental influences, and both emphasised a need for all of us to learn how to manage hurt and disappointment as part of normal human experience. In this sense there is also some resemblance to Albert Bandura's social learning theory (1971) and Lev Vygotsky's (1987) socio-cultural theory in which the environment is explicitly or implicitly considered a crucial mechanism in development. Likewise, the sociologist Urie Bronfenbrenner (1974) developed ecological systems theory, which views child development as a complex system of relationships affected by multiple levels of the surrounding environment, from the immediate settings of family and school to broad cultural values, laws and customs. In this way, he showed that the immediate familial environment is shaped and influenced by wider societal values, social policy, the law of the land, economics, and the way that global, local and familial developments influence each other. In short, our understanding of children and their development is complicated by the environment they are growing up in, and the ways in which familial and societal influences are shaped by nation state, global laws and cultural values. This is a lot to take in and convey, and perhaps because of this it can become easier to overlook complexity in our work with children.

The problem with becoming an expert in only one or two theories

While running the meditation project with some teenage girls in a British secondary school, I was struck by the damage that is caused by professionals and carers bandying around weighty terms without thinking through their impact. At the time I had known the girls for two years, since Year 7, and among their group Amber was generally quite upbeat and popular, despite managing a complex home life which included continuous social work involvement. Over the two years that I knew her she had become more trusting and able to focus in class, and had begun to appreciate that bullying takes many forms and that aggressive retaliation towards bullies could also be considered a bullying response. She felt confident in herself, had stopped responding like with like to aggressive peers, and was using the meditative methods that we had developed to good effect in and out of school. I had become used to her bouncing confidently into our sessions... and so it was a shock to see her turn up to our session one day close to tears and very downbeat. Rather than chat and jolly along the group, she sat in silence until it was her turn to speak, at which point she mumbled with tears rolling down her face: '*I'm really upset, my social worker has told me and my mum that I am suffering from anxiety, and now I do not know what to do... everyone is worried, my mum is crying, and my social worker has said it is really serious.*'

This was incredibly out of character, and because I knew Amber quite well by this stage, I did not immediately refer to her '*anxiety*' and instead asked if she would be happy to talk about events in the run up to the social work visit. It turned out that her mum had made the very difficult decision to ask her stepfather to move out. On hearing this, the girls in the group expressed sympathy and I went on to ask how Amber's mum and siblings were doing. Amber explained that she had taken charge of the family meals so that her mum, who was inconsolable, could rest. Amber had looked after her younger siblings, got them ready for school, cooked in the evenings and had stayed up late into the night comforting her mum. When the social worker had arrived at the house, Amber had finally felt able to relax and express some of her pent-up sorrow, and her mum, meanwhile, perhaps buoyed up by her daughter's on-going support, had been able to rally at Amber's side. I think that the girls in the group were as impressed as I was by Amber's capacity to step up and care for her family, and we could all see that she was both exhausted and understandably sad.

After asking Amber if she would like to hear my reflections on the week's events, I reflected on whether it might not be too unexpected for her to be feeling tired, fraught and sad in the aftermath of such an unexpected turn of events. I also reflected that, from my perspective, she had also shown an admirable strength of character by stepping up to care for her mum and brothers and sister. I praised her capacity to be so caring, and invited the other girls in the group to share their thoughts. After a while Amber brightened up considerably, sat tall and said, '*maybe I'm not anxious?*' We all nodded and went on to talk about the importance of giving ourselves time and space to feel emotions such as sadness, fear and grief.

When Amber's social worker paid her a visit, she unfortunately drew upon her training in mental health not to offer thoughtful and person-centred support but to label Amber in a way that made Amber feel inadequate and incomplete. The intervention was poorly thought through, was shoddily executed and did nothing to improve Amber's sense of well-being. It follows that if we are properly listened to, cared for and treated with love and kindness, then we are likely to develop positive self-worth and have the mental space to enjoy going about our daily lives feeling secure enough to be interested in the wider world and open to new experiences. The humanist psychologist Carl Rogers (1951) coined this experience one of '*unconditional positive regard*'. Rogers recognised the importance of being cared for in this way and understood that it is through the simple act of showing compassionate and non-judgemental loving kindness that people are most likely to develop secure attachments to each other and the professionals who care for them, and in turn be able to move out into their wider world with a strong sense of self and a quiet confidence in themselves.

Better forms of communication

The challenge of communicating these ideas to lay people remains. There are some very useful visual aids, such as the Circle of Security approach developed by Marvin et al (2002), who produced a visual aid to show, as part of a 20-week parenting training programme, what secure attachments look like in practice. Their Circle of Security can be discussed and shared in a non-judgemental and supportive way in a wide variety of settings, including with children and young people.

Circle of Security
Caregiver Attending To The Child's Needs

I need you to...

Support My Exploration

Watch Over Me
Delight In Me
Help Me
Enjoy With Me

SECURE BASE

I need you to...

SAFE HAVEN
- Protect Me
- Comfort Me
- Delight In Me
- Organize My Feelings

Welcome My Coming To You

Always: be Bigger, Stronger, Wiser, and Kind
Whenever possible: follow my child's need
Whenever necessary: take charge

© 2018 Cooper, Hoffman, and Powell; Circle of Security International

Figure 2.1 *Circle of security*

Developing this form of mind-mindedness seems to be key to our capacity for empathy. This can become difficult to sustain if members of a family are constantly alert to possible threats and ill-treatment, either from wider society or from individuals whom they live with. It also becomes challenging to behave in a calm and measured way for people who have also experienced their own challenges and mistreatment while growing up.

Our response to uncertainty and mistreatment: the fight or flight response

The American paediatrician Nadine Burke Harris (2018) provides a useful analogy when explaining why growing up in an unpredictable home environment is so damaging to us:

> *...imagine you are in a wood and a bear appears, your heart starts thumping, your blood flows with adrenalin, and your frontal lobes of the brain become flooded with cortisol, making you ready to either run (very fast) from the bear or fight it.*

You are hard wired to fight that bear. But what if an adult in your family is that bear and comes at you every day? In other words, how do repeated stressors affect a child's development and what are the long-term effects?

Physical effects of stress

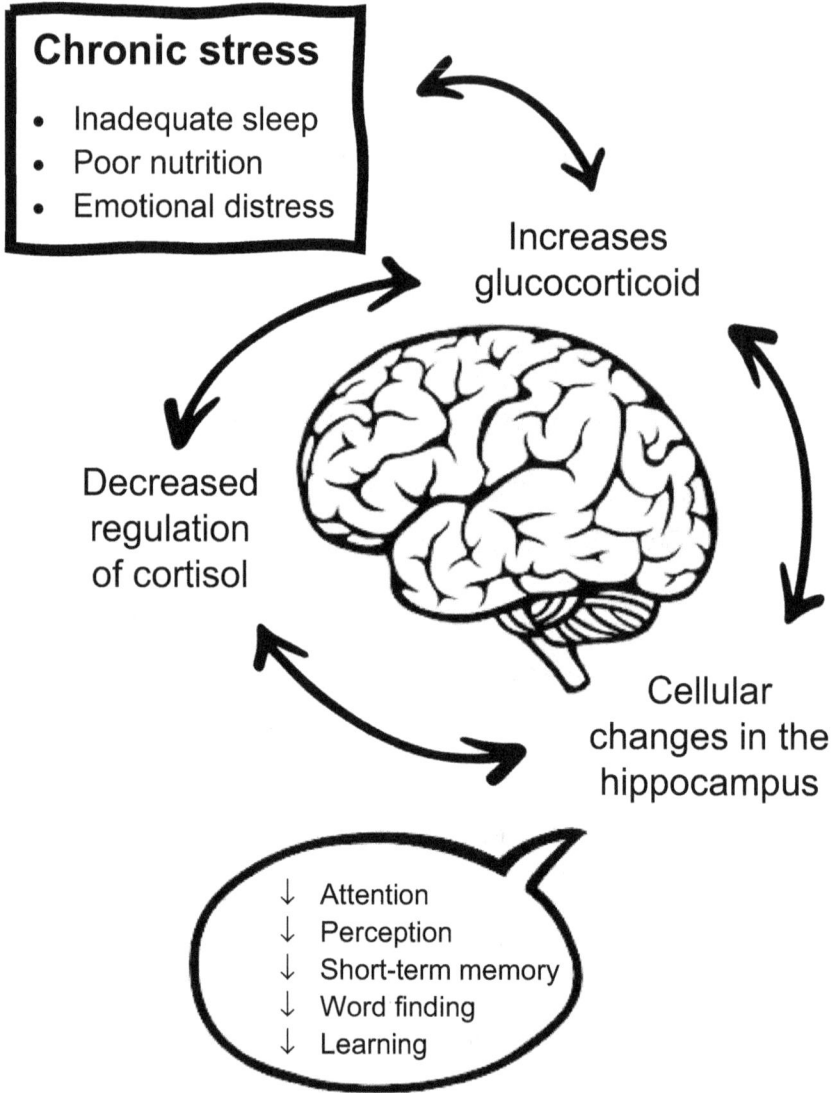

Figure 2.2 *The stress-brain loop*

When we experience a stressful event, the amygdala, an area of the brain that contributes to emotional processing, sends a distress signal to the hypothalamus and cortisol is released. After the amygdala sends a distress signal, the hypothalamus activates the sympathetic nervous system by sending signals through the autonomic nerves to the adrenal glands. These glands respond by pumping the hormone epinephrine (also known as adrenaline) into the bloodstream. As epinephrine circulates through the body, it brings on a number of physiological changes. Sight, hearing and other senses become sharper. Even babies living in high-conflict homes experience a pronounced spike in activity in the rostral anterior cortex, a region associated with the processing of emotion, and one that is frequently altered among people suffering from stress disorders.

Infants and young children, like older children living under similar circumstances, experience heightened activity in more primitive areas of the brain and have permanently elevated cortisol levels. Elevated cortisol levels result in children over-reacting to daily events, no matter the context. The child who goes from sitting calmly in school to flying off the handle when challenged may well be doing so because their baseline cortisol is already at fight/flight levels, making it extremely difficult for them to control their emotions, to focus or stay calm, or to engage in conversation in a measured manner. These findings have contributed to trauma-based understanding of human behaviour. Trauma-based work is helpful for our understanding of how and *why* the children and young people we work with might be struggling to hold themselves in check, and might not respond with immediacy to standard forms of intervention and support.

The rise of trauma-informed practice

The trauma model also helps us understand the on-going impact of ill-treatment (often long after the events have passed, as in the case of Beth, referred to previously). Widespread use of the term can partly be attributed to wide publicity and coverage of the CDC-Kaiser Permanente Adverse Childhood Experiences (ACEs) study, which focuses on the long-term impact of childhood abuse and neglect and household challenges on later-life health and well-being. The original ACE study was conducted at Kaiser Permanente, USA from 1995 to 1997. Its findings garnered international recognition because they showed a direct link between childhood neglect, impaired cognitive development and poor long-term physical health outcomes (see Felitti et al, 1998).

In other words, if a person experiences physical and emotional deprivation during childhood they are far more likely to develop life-threatening conditions such as heart disease and cancer. The findings are significant because they show that when we grow up in households where parenting is inconsistent and sometimes threatening, and the environment is unpredictable, we not only absorb the hurt, but we internalise it to such a degree that it can make us physically unwell. As a result, the CDC-Kaiser ACEs study came out with a list of high-risk markers relating to factors such as divorce, having a parent with mental health issues and substance misuse, and concluded that the higher the ACEs score the more likely a person is to internalise health-threatening traumas. It is this aspect of the CDC-Kaiser study that is central to the genesis of this book.

In the past we might have had a sense that stressful home lives or unexpected life events such as the death of a parent were emotionally damaging, but we now have the evidence to show that even the very youngest babies can be very much affected. This discovery has resulted in keen interest in the CDC-Kaiser ACEs study, so much so that some local authorities in the UK are now adopting trauma-informed practice as their central approach for work with children. But how valid is this? Should we be allowing one model to take dominance? Or would it be more appropriate to include it within a wide armoury of expert approaches? I suggest the latter because, as with other approaches, the trauma model also has some limitations.

Critics point out that ACEs scores only examine the negative influences in a person's life and do not also examine positive experiences in early life that can help build resilience and protect a child from the effects of trauma. As Jack Shonkoff (2016, p 32), a paediatrician and director of the Center on the Developing Child at Harvard University, has also pointed out, '*There are people with high ACE scores who do remarkably well*'. Katy Hetherington, writing for Public Health Scotland (2020), argues that we should not conflate childhood adversity with trauma. Adversity is broader than trauma, and traumatic events in childhood are one form of childhood adversity. However, not all childhood adversity is traumatic. Instead, we can decrease risk by supporting trauma-informed principles of enabling people we work with to experience choice, collaboration, safety and trust.

Finding fault

In general, psychology and child development leans towards a deficit model in which the focus is on damage that has been built up in a person's life. This is the case whether we embrace a trauma- or attachment-based framework for understanding emotional development. In this sense, as Maté (2019) has pointed out, the dominant approach is to decide '*what is wrong with a person*' and to provide a clinical diagnosis and prescribe a standardised form of intervention, such as a generic course of mindfulness practice or a prescription drug, but not to go on to ask the diagnosed person '*why is this happening to you?*', or to think about the individual's experiences in the context of interconnected influences based on parenting style, where they live and their family's standard of living. Others, such as Peele and Thompson (2014), have been critical of Maté's overt focus on trauma, and like me, Peele thinks that we should support people in the broadest sense. While reviewing Maté's ideas, Peele argues that the focus on past trauma depletes people's confidence, energy and belief in the possibility that they can overcome trauma and deal with immediate life and emotional problems. His analogy echoes my feelings about how Amber was treated by her social worker.

As a mind experiment, imagine answering a call from a person considering suicide. Who in their right mind would say: '*Imagine the worst thing that has happened in your life, and keep that as your main focus going forward*'?

Putting ideas into practice

A starting point could be to avoid diagnostic interpretation of behaviour and replace overly focused references to resilience, well-being, trauma and attachment-informed therapy with straightforward support that children and their carers can relate to.

Signs of Safety

The Signs of Safety approach (1990s) developed in Australia by Andrew Turnell and Steve Edwards, two practising social workers, takes a whole-family approach to supporting positive change. There are also some thoughtful examples from outside academic and professional circles for young children and their carers to tap in to. The books of children's writer Judith Kerr depict children living lives that the reader can relate to and be reassured by. Take *The Tiger Who Came to Tea* (1968), a thrilling tale that grips the attention of young readers: will the tiger gobble up the little girl and her mother? Or will their story become the most extraordinary of adventures? At its heart it is a book depicting a loving mother quietly protecting her child from unexpected danger and reframing an unexpected threat as a piece of fun. Crucially, it also shows children that life can be unpredictable, and that it is the parents' job to be a source of stability and calm and to create a sense of safety. It is a very reassuring book for young children and their parents or carers to read, and a book that I have shared and worked through with families in my role as a social worker.

More than anything, I like the light-touch approach adopted by Judith Kerr. Her book provides simple visuals to open up discussion, and show that how people respond to children shapes their internal world, what they think about themselves and how they should gauge the behaviour of those they encounter. There are other books that are just as useful and just as much fun; Trish Cooke and Helen Oxenbury's book *So Much* (2008) is a lovely tale which can also be used to highlight the importance of being able to put oneself in the shoes of the children in our care, and take the time to imagine how they see the world and us.

Psychology of happiness

As the psychologist Martin Seligman, a pioneer of positive psychology, has stated, since the Second World War the field of psychology has largely focused on suffering and how to formally measure previously unclear experiences such as depression and schizophrenia. It has not examined what gives people a sense of fulfilment and contentment nor has it focused on why some people overcome difficult childhood experiences. Through the use of questionnaires, Seligman and his co-author Christopher Peterson found that the most satisfied, upbeat people were those who had discovered their unique combination of 'signature strengths', such as humanity, temperance and persistence (Peterson and Seligman, 2004). This vision of happiness echoes the virtue ethics of ancient philosophers such as that of the Chinese philosopher Confucius, who placed value on individuals acting for the greater good of the collective over that of the individual (Burr, 2006). Seligman's conclusion is that happiness has three dimensions that can be cultivated: the pleasant life, the good life and the meaningful life.

The pleasant life is realised if we learn to savour and appreciate such basic pleasures as companionship, the natural environment and our bodily needs. According to modern theories of self-esteem, life is only genuinely satisfying if we discover value within ourselves. The good life recognises that one of the best ways of discovering this value is by nourishing our unique strengths in contributing to the happiness of our fellow humans.

Consequently, the final stage is the meaningful life, in which we find a deep sense of ful-filment by employing our unique strengths for a purpose greater than ourselves.

Seligman's theory reconciles two conflicting views of human happiness: the individual-istic approach, which emphasises that we should take care of ourselves and nurture our own strengths, and the altruistic approach, which tends to downplay individuality and emphasises sacrifice for the greater purpose. Doing good for and by others creates greater contentment and also takes us out of ourselves. The same applies whatever our personal circumstances.

Neurology and its contribution

While I was living and working in Vietnam, I watched monks quietly garner strength through meditative practice, and saw some of the street and working children that I worked with draw comfort from placing offerings on an ancestral worship table in their orphanage. I also started visiting a pagoda to light incense with some of the young boys who worked on the streets. During our visits we would sit together in meditative thought. I learnt so much from those boys and also from the Catholic priest, Father Charlie, who I was working alongside at the children's re-education detention centre. There I observed that older boys who showed kindness to others had the highest standing. The same group of boys wore a tattoo that read '*I have no money, I have no freedom, I have no love, but one day I will have those things again*'. It was a tattoo of strength and hope (Burr, 2006).

Far later, having worked with children in England, I learnt that there was a growing interest in mindfulness and meditative practice. I came across the work of Sara Lazar (2011), a neurologist based at Harvard, who has been documenting a link between regular meditative practice and neurological recovery, particularly in the frontal lobes and the amygdala, an area that, as Nadine Burke Harris has pointed out, is so detrimentally affected by on-going abuse and damage. The idea that the neurological damage caused by trauma does not have to be permanent is central to Lazar's findings. Once she made this discovery by regularly scanning her own brain and documenting changes to her frontal lobes, she went on to do brain scans using magnetic resonance images (MRI) on members of the population who either did or did not practise meditation on a regular basis. She found that it was only among those who meditated that frontal lobe recovery took place (McGreevey, 2011). I was very struck by her findings because of my child protection and human rights interests and work as a social worker and anthropologist. On discovering Lazar's ideas, I started to introduce medi-tative practice to my children with a view to possibly doing something similar with teenagers, because like the Children's Commissioner for England and Robbie Duschinsky (referred to earlier) I know that this age group is often poorly supported when it comes to addressing their emotional development.

Perhaps because of my interest in meditation, one of my sons, who was then aged six, independently decided to set up a meditation club under the bushes by the edge of his school playground as a way of escaping play-time noise and chaos. Meanwhile, a few years later, another son of mine, who knew about my work with children, cheekily responded to classroom-based mindfulness practice by purposely eating the raisin he had been asked to focus on because he recognised that in staring at the raisin he was also being tested on his self-control, and as a result of talking to me was well versed in Walter Mischel's Stanford marshmallow test (Mischel and Grusec, 1967).

Limitations of mindfulness practice

My hunch was that there was something in all of this that could be restorative for vulnerable young people, but an approach dominated by a standardised approach to mindfulness, which was gaining popularity in schools, could be limiting. From my observations, mindfulness tended to focus on the individual's journey towards happiness without also overtly incorporating and encouraging active altruism and kindness towards members of the wider community. This meant that, at its worst, it could be used as a self-serving route to happiness.

Yet I could see from Seligman's work that deeper life satisfaction (rather than happiness) comes from leading a meaningful life that touches the lives of others. While Lazar's work on meditation demonstrates that people who regularly practise tend to become more generous over time, her findings focus on the outcome for adults and not for children, and particularly children who have been affected by abuses of various kinds. I also felt that some of the more generic aspects of mindfulness practice that are introduced into schools do not consider the potential that there are children who are experiencing abuse sitting in their audience.

If abuse takes place in the home, it is likely to occur in the private domain of a child's bedroom, and in the dark. When we close our eyes, we make ourselves vulnerable. With this last point in mind, I believe that there should be far more caution and preparation put into working with children and teenagers. It is irresponsible for any practitioner to instruct members of an audience to close their eyes without also knowing that they feel comfortable to do so. We should also hold, contain and continually root the people whom we support so that they stay in the present throughout the process.

Key thoughts

Despite having theories to hand that remind us that we cannot work properly with children and young people unless we consider the wider context in which they are being raised, we still tend to respond to children at the individual level, as highlighted by Amber's, Mia's and Beth's experiences. Wider influences that also shape our sense of self are often sidelined. For example, social workers are currently well-versed in attachment theories and trauma-based models of intervention, while teachers are better versed in social pedagogic theories and ideas about cognitive development. Schools tend to adopt behaviourist strategies to control children, while social workers and counsellors are more likely to draw upon psychodynamic theories to understand the same behaviours. Used alone, these deficit-based models pathologise the nature of human existence.

Where we once referred to attachment-based interventions and resilience, the current focus is now on emotional well-being and 'trauma-informed' support. Yet there is no reason why one approach should dominate or be introduced to supersede past methods of understanding childhood experiences. Instead, it would be more useful to draw upon a range of interventions and practices, and to think about them not only in terms of their widespread application and level of integrated contribution, but also in terms of their cultural relevance.

In short, our medically informed practice currently leans towards a deficit model of the human psyche in which a diagnosis is applied to deal with discontent and unhappiness, while failing to address wider structural reasons that might be contributing to people feeling unhappy. When these quick fixes, all of which are centred on individual diagnosis, fail to work, or a child seems unhappy, we treat the child as the problem, and pathologise rather than legitimise their experiences (as happened with the social worker in Amber's case). It is time to put children and young people centre stage, and to move away from interventions based on swift diagnosis and the medication of any signs of distress.

Why group work is so beneficial

We should try to sit alongside children and young people to properly learn about their circumstances, and work with them using techniques that support the development of their own personalised emotional toolkit. To do this properly it is important to create the space for each child or young person to voice their emotions, both one on one (if necessary), and in small group settings. Peer-to-peer-based group settings are key to the practices we developed. Children and young people gain comfort from recognising that they are not alone in what they are experiencing, and that other young people also have similar feelings to theirs. They also gain satisfaction from being in group setting in which they are encouraged to think about other people's feelings and be both supportive and kind to others.

References

Adams, T (2021) Judith Kerr Was Right, Time Flies for Adults, But Childhood Lasts Half a Lifetime. *The Guardian*, 9 May. [online] Available at: www.theguardian.com/commentisfree/2021/may/09/judith-kerr-right-times-flies-for-adults (accessed 18 June 2022).

Bandura, A (1971) *Social Learning Theory*. New York: General Learning Press.

Beckett, C and Taylor, H (2019) *Human Growth and Development*. London: Sage.

Bowlby, J (1971) *Attachment and Loss (Vol. 1: Attachment)*. 1st ed. London: Penguin Books.

Bronfenbrenner, U (1974) Developmental Research, Public Policy, and the Ecology of Childhood. *Child Development*, 45(1): 1–5.

Burke Harris, N (2018) *The Deepest Well: Healing the Long-Term Effects of Childhood Adversity*. London: Bluebird.

Burr, R (2006) *Vietnam's Children in a Changing World*. Chicago: Rutgers.

Cooke, T and Oxenbury, H (2008) *So Much*. London: Walker Books.

Dalai Lama and Cutler, C (1998) *The Art of Happiness: A Handbook for Living*. London: Hodder & Stoughton.

Dunn, J and Kendrick, C (1982) *Siblings: Love, Envy and Understanding*. Cambridge, MA: Harvard University Press.

Duschinsky, R (2020) *Cornerstones of Attachment Research*. Oxford: Oxford University Press.

Duschinsky, R and Reijman, S (2016) Filming Disorganised Attachment. *Screen*, 57(4): 397–413.

Duschinsky, R and Solomon, J (2017) Infant Disorganised Attachment: Clarifying Levels of Analysis. *Clinical Child Psychology*, 22(4): 524–38.

Ellis, B (2010) *Bad Things in the Night*. London: Ebury.

Erikson, E (1968) *Identity: Youth and Crisis*. New York: Norton.

Felitti,V J, Anda, R F, Nordenberg, D, Williamson, D F, Spitz, A M, Edwards, V, Koss, M P and Marks, J S (1998) Relationship of Childhood Abuse and Household Dysfunction to Many of the Leading Causes of Death in Adults. The Adverse Childhood Experiences (ACE) Study. *American Journal of Preventive Medicine*, 14(4): 245–58.

Freud, A and Dann, S (1951) An Experiment in Group Upbringing. *Psychoanalytic Study of the Child*, 6: 127–68.

Freud, S ([1933] 2013). *The Interpretation of Dreams*. London: Macmillan.

Hetherington, K, on behalf of PHS Scotland (2020) *Ending Childhood Diversity: A Public Health Approach*. Edinburgh: OGL.

Kerr, J (1968) *The Tiger Who Came to Tea*. London: HarperCollins.

Klein, M (1923) The Development of a Child. *International Journal of Psycho-Analysis*, 4: 419–74.

Lazer, S (2011) How Meditation Can Reshape Our Brains. TED Talk at Cambridge.

Marvin, R, Cooper, G, Hoffman, K and Powell, B (2002) *Circle of Security Intervention: Enhancing Attachment in Early Parent-Child Relationships*. New York: Guilford Press.

Maté, G (2019) *When the Body Says No: The Cost of Hidden Stress*. London: Vermillion.

McGreevey, S (2011) Eight Weeks to a Better Brain. *The Harvard Gazette*, 21 January. [online] Available at: https://news.harvard.edu/gazette/story/2011/01/eight-weeks-to-a-better-brain (accessed 18 June 2022).

Mischel, W and Grusec, J (1967) Waiting for Rewards and Punishments. Effects of Time and Probability on Choice. *Journal of Personality and Social Psychology*, 5(1): 24–31.

Peele, S and Thompson, I (2014) *Recover! Stop Thinking Like an Addict and Reclaim Your Life with The PERFECT Program*. Boston, MA: De Capo.

Peterson, C and Seligman, M (2004) *Character Strengths and Virtues: A Handbook and Classification*. Oxford: Oxford University Press.

Piaget, J (1950) *The Psychology of Intelligence*. London: Routledge.

Rogers, C (1951) *Client-Centered Therapy: Its Current Practice, Implications and Theory*. London: Constable.

Shonkoff, J P (2016) Capitalizing on Advances in Science to Reduce the Health Consequences of Early Childhood Adversity. *JAMA Pediatrics*, 170(10): 1003–7.

Vygotsky, L S (1987) *The Collected Works of L. S. Vygotsky: Vol. 1. Problems of General Psychology*. New York: Plenum.

3 Current approaches to mental health

If you miss being understood by laymen, and fail to put your hearers in this condition, you will miss reality.

Hippocrates (*On Ancient Medicine*)

Today the subject of young people's mental health is a regular topic of public discussion. There seems to be growing societal consensus that a significant number of children and young people are likely, at some point, to struggle with psychological difficulties. However, as individuals with a vested interest in the subject of childhood and youth, it is important that we closely examine contemporary ideas about the state of children's mental health, and in particular the proposition that poor mental health is on the rise. In short, we need to understand context if we are to work effectively with children.

This chapter explores the current thinking on the subject, the influences shaping our ideas and expectations for children and young people experiencing mental health issues, and the extent to which reactions to emotional challenges in childhood are shaped by a combination of environmental and cultural influences. It looks at how societal expectations have an effect on how people think about and express themselves, the dominant ideas about mental health and the forms of diagnosis and treatments currently in vogue. It concludes by examining how societal forces and the availability of health services shape the extent to which we are able to seek support during times of need and the form that that support takes.

The impact of Covid-19 on mental health and well-being

Not surprisingly, the Covid-19 pandemic has added a new dimension to our growing interest in the state of our children's mental health. At the height of the pandemic the majority of children and young people were not able to attend school, and spent time at home, either alone or in close proximity to other family members. The general consensus is that this was challenging for most of us, but that children growing up in low-income families with limited online resources were far more negatively affected than other members of the population. Evidence shows that domestic violence was on the rise and that children growing up in abusive environments were not able to access their normal channels of support. There was also concern about the long-term effect of a widening attainment gap experienced by children from the most disadvantaged backgrounds (Creswell et al, 2020).

Unexpected outcomes

Yet while valid concerns were raised about the impact on children of being isolated from their wider community and from protective influences outside the home, there was also parallel and under-reported coverage of some of the unexpected benefits of lockdown for a minority of children. It seems that, despite the challenges, some of the most anxious children thrived and were happier in lockdown than during normal circumstances (Oosterhoff et al, 2020). A study run by the University of Oxford found that secondary school children felt less worried and happier while at home with their families, and a study run by Essex University reported that parents felt that they were now closer to their children. Why might some children and young people not only have been happier but also purported to be unexpectedly free from symptoms of anxiety during a global pandemic that was generally acknowledged to be creating widespread societal distress? More importantly, what, within their normal, pre-pandemic, day-to-day experiences, had been creating such high levels of disharmony? In short, what did the pandemic remove some children and young people from? Are there environmental factors that are making them unwell? How is their expression of anxiety received by the people around them? We will explore these questions in detail, but for now let's examine the types of mental health conditions associated with children and young people.

Typical diagnosis

In the UK, when children and teenagers are diagnosed with mental health conditions they are typically categorised as having anxiety, attention deficit hyperactivity disorder (ADHD) or low-level depression. Younger children are more likely to be diagnosed with ADHD, and pre-teens and teenagers are most likely to be treated for anxiety or depression with underlying influences. Circumstantial evidence indicates that this split in diagnosis through the developmental ages is linked to changing circumstances. Our formal education system expects young children to spend a great deal of time in classroom settings concentrating and sitting still, in ways that do not come easy to everyone. Depression and anxiety in the teenage years can also be linked to school- and parent-created exam pressures, alongside physiological and hormonal changes. In addition, some representations of behavioural distress are associated with other conditions, such as autism.

Yet it should be acknowledged that conditions such as anxiety, depression, ADHD, autism and attachment disorders are not treated by the psychiatric profession as mutually exclusive from each other. Children who enter formal mental health services may receive a range of separate diagnoses across the course of their childhoods. There is increasing evidence that young people with ADHD have a high tendency to move on to being diagnosed with depression during their adolescence and substantial overlap has been reported between ADHD and autism spectrum disorder (ASD). In 2019, Madjar et al published the results from a 12-year longitudinal study of 6380 children prescribed methylphenidate for ADHD between the ages of six and eight years old, reporting that of the group 50 per cent subsequently went on to receive anti-depressants during adolescence. In other words, taking medication for ADHD provided a starting point for long-term pharmaceutical drug use for a significant number of young people in the cohort. According to Boyle (2011), the last 20 years have seen steady increases in the estimated prevalence of both ASD and ADHD in childhood. In this regard the UK is not alone: this rise in child-associated 'disorders' has been documented across the northern hemisphere, in places as diverse as the United States, France, Norway, the Netherlands and the UK. If we are to properly help such affected children, we need to understand why this is happening and what, if anything, we can do to support them actively and positively.

If we refer back to Chapter 1, we can also link these medicalised forms of intervention to our expectations of children's lives being increasingly dominated by a narrowing of what a 'normal' and 'acceptable' childhood looks like. Over the last 150 years there has been a seismic shift in the 'jobs' that children do. Few of them now growing up in post-industrial societies need to enter the labour market; instead, it is 'their' job during their early years to reignite experiences of escape, play and innocence, in the immediate sphere of their families, and later excel in exams so that they become successful and fulfil 'their' potential. In this way, societal shifts in expectation could be interpreted as narrowing and limiting our expectations for children and young people. In reality, it does not take very much for any child to fail to live up to what is required of them. If we factor in the additional challenges faced by children entering our education settings who perhaps enjoy solitude, or were premature, or have chaotic home lives, then it is easy to start to think differently about what might be informing their disquiet and whether our education system is too focused on formal academic achievement.

Having proposed that the social construction of childhood is driven by wider cultural forces, we can in the same vein discuss different ways to think about and explore a medicalised diagnostic approach to human suffering. We have critically examined basic assumptions about a 'good' childhood; there is also value in stepping back to reflect upon wider societal influences that might also shape how children and young people are understood and treated. So, rather than take this apparent rise in psychiatric distress at face value, it is worth exploring alternative perspectives.

Wider considerations

Perhaps the actual numbers of children and young people experiencing difficulties has not changed at all. Rather, it might be that our engagement with our emotions is focused on particular forms of expression shaped by wider and continually evolving societal influences. With this thought in mind, we can turn to recent history to evidence a shifting language of emotion and meaning across the centuries. As the author Lesley Hartley wrote in his book *The Go-Between*, '*the past is a foreign country; they do things differently there*' (Hartley, 1953, p 1). And doing things differently is exactly the point; as the following example highlights, the experience of loss and pain does not alter, but the expression of these emotions does.

My grandparents' loss

As a child, I recall the stoicism with which my grandma alluded to the impact of the Second World War. When I was about seven years old, she and I had sat down together to polish the brass from the mantle in her living room. That morning the sun was streaming in through the open window, and my grandma was kneeling close beside me, her tweed skirt pulled tight over her knees. I recall both being very taken by the delicate hammer markings running across the surface of a delicate little copper bowl that I was polishing and being keenly struck by my grandma's disquiet when I asked about its origin. Even as a young child I could sense pain in her reaction, and felt the atmosphere of harmony shift as she took time to collect herself, to look down, to adjust and smooth the creases in her skirt in a bid to constrain her emotions. The sun still streamed through the window and time seemingly stood still, as it so often does in such moments. Her simple one sentence response was '*it was made by your grandad's friend who fought alongside him in the war*'. And that was all. So, with the light innocence of a child I asked if they were still friends, and was told that while reconnoitring a field together in Italy, my grandad's friend had spotted a land mine and jumped on it in order to save the men around him. I remember, as a seven year old, sensing the enormous sadness of that event, of sitting on the rug by the fire and holding the bowl, and thinking of the bravery of a man who had no doubt saved my grandfather's life. In my grandma's brief response, the loss was very palpable. There was no doubt in my young mind that the copper bowl was symbolic of the largest sacrifice that anyone could make, and no more words were needed or could have properly expressed how my grandma was feeling.

Today she might have expressed her sadness differently. She might have chosen to give an evasive response, in case the story of a man's death was too much for a child to hear and the knowledge of a violent death would traumatise me in some way. As suggested previously, contemporary childhood exists in a culture of overt protection and use of extreme forms of language to express emotion. The language of emotion has shifted and become more urgent and crisis driven, and also linked to a Western medicalised understanding of the human psyche. Children growing up in contemporary Britain are encouraged to be well versed in the language of emotion associated with expressions of anxiety and trauma.

Anxiety and trauma

This shift towards an 'anxiety' and 'trauma' based model of emotion has been thoroughly documented and pinpointed in time and place. Barclay et al (2020) point out that among historians studying changes in expression of emotion, eighteenth-century Europe has been associated with a '*culture of sensibility*', while '*the age of anxiety*' denotes emotions of the post 9/11 West. This shift also reflects what I have witnessed in my work as a social worker, when prior to 9/11 (roughly between 1992 and 2000) children's emotions were discussed in terms of their capacity for resilience. We did not have the language of emotional well-being or trauma to hand; those terms had not come into being in the way that we understand and apply them today. Likewise, there was little interest in attachment theory (see Chapter 2) as the starting point for thinking about the quality of children's lives, nor in any impact familial relationships might have on mental health.

This idea that our expression of emotions is continually evolving is a helpful one to consider, and creates new points of reference. When I speak to children and young people and they tell me that they are worried or anxious or traumatised in some way, I first want to find out what the term means to them, and where the idea that they are experiencing such difficulties has come from. Otherwise, how can I have a proper meeting of minds with the children to whom I offer support?

Mental health and the importance of language

We need to be able to understand words and their meaning if we are to successfully express ourselves, communicate with other people and create common meaning between individuals and groups. Yet, even within one generation of people, if we are to really understand each other we need to choose our words carefully and draw upon language that is culture-specific and contextual. Clear communication is at the heart of meaningful relationships, and when we hear what other people are saying we assume that our interpretation of their meaning is accurate, that what we associate with their words properly reflects what they intended to say, and also what they intended for us to hear. Consequently, we often make the mistake of presuming commonality not only in the present but across different cultures, in terms of both how we express emotion and how we diagnose conditions. Arthur Kleinman, who was both a medical anthropologist and physician, pointed out that the Western approach needs to categorise human experience in purely medical terms. For example 'heart discomfort' for Iranians is not the equivalent of 'heart palpitations' for Americans; it does not mean the same thing (Goody, 1977).

I first came across the discipline of medical anthropology while I was training to become a social worker. At the time I was on a hospital placement as a student at the Royal Brompton hospital in central London. During the placement I was asked to run a support group for people waiting for or recovering from heart and/or lung transplants. The group was made up of men and women from all walks of life, and from a medical perspective the aim of the meetings was to prepare people for pragmatic life-saving medical procedures. It offered far more than that. One of the group members was an 18-year-old woman from South Africa who had heart failure. I was warned that she was emotionally unstable and unpredictable. One of my social work colleagues told me that she had grandiose delusions about her position in life and was very demanding. When I finally met the young girl, I interpreted her behaviour differently. Instead, I saw her as someone who, in what should have been the prime of her life, was instead facing life-threatening uncertainty, living far away from home, and sitting in fearful limbo, not knowing if she was going to receive a lifesaving organ. Yet because she had been labelled as mentally unstable, I was also told that she was not in favour with the transplant team. Just before the end of my placement I built up the courage to speak up on behalf of this young girl, and talked about how I might have behaved if my life choices had been so cruelly constrained at such a young age. As a consequence, we revisited the diagnosis of the young woman and concluded that her feelings of distress were not pathological but might be caused by feelings of powerlessness brought on by living in a limbo state.

Likewise, when I was qualified, my first position involved working in A & E at Charing Cross Hospital. On one occasion, a young Somalian woman was referred to our duty team for further support. The psychiatrist explained that the woman had been formally sectioned (which means she should not leave the hospital) because she was psychotic, evidenced by signs of continual distress and a phantom pregnancy. At the time of referral, she had already been in hospital for a week and was medicated. Yet she had only been treated by members of the medical profession, none of whom spoke her language. My first action was to organise a translator and to recommend that one of us meet the woman with a female member of her tribal group present. During our meeting the young woman confirmed that she was in deep mourning for her deceased husband and unborn child, who she had lost while fleeing a rebel attack to her village. She was visibly relieved to be speaking with someone who understood the real and acute source of her distress and the psychiatrist's diagnosis was lifted.

Conditions and diagnoses explained

As shown above, part of a medical approach is to diagnose using a standard set of criteria. In a paper examining preventative psychiatry, McCrory et al (2017) point out that, over the last 20 years, the field of child mental health has been increasingly organised around a medical model with a focus on seeking to investigate diagnosable psychiatric disorders. The options open to children and their families have also narrowed to access via the GP, who can make a referral to CAMHS (Child and Adolescent Mental Health Services) and to school counsellors. Some positive voluntary resources are also available via organisations such as NHS IRock or Time to Talk, but all services are framed around the distress of the individual, and interventions begin and end with *the language of diagnosis*.

In the UK, guidelines are set by the National Institute for Health and Care Excellence (NICE) set up by central government in 1999 with a remit to make evidence-based recommendations about particular medical conditions and their treatment. Since then, NICE guidelines have become internationally influential and, unless appropriately contested, are often viewed as representing the gold standard of medical practice. NICE currently approaches both depression and ADHD with medication as the starting point and published a guideline on the treatment of ADHD in September 2008. The guideline concluded that both childhood and adulthood ADHD were 'valid' diagnoses and recommended that stimulant drugs should be the initial treatment for all adults with ADHD and children with the most severe symptoms (Moncrieff and Timimi, 2013). However, what is meant by 'severe' is very much open to interpretation, as echoed in the work of medical anthropologists such as Arthur Kleinman (1988). The increasing popularity of clinical guidelines reflects political changes in Western systems of healthcare delivery, the changing nature of professional power and the manner in which such guidelines rank certain forms of knowledge and research designs above others (Goldenberg, 2006; Lambert, 2006).

Creating attention deficit hyperactivity disorder

Before 1968, when the precursor of ADHD first appeared in the international *Diagnostic and Statistical Manual of Mental Disorders* (DSM), restless children with a short attention span still existed but were instead recognised as victims of a condition known as 'neurasthenia', which literally means 'weak nerves'. They were also understood to find formal study challenging, and might have been removed from academic schools into more relaxed educational settings. In some more enlightened school environments similar interventions still take place today, as reflected in a body of research that myself and colleagues at the University of Sussex completed for the England Children's Commissioner on the subject of enhanced well-being among secondary school pupils. Our findings showed that where the school regimes were child centred, students reported feeling more emotionally robust, regardless of family background. In one instance the headmaster of a grammar school had successfully kept a bright but restless 15-year-old boy in school by creating an opportunity for him to complete an apprenticeship in a garage alongside studying for GCSEs. The end result was that the teenager stayed engaged in his studies and was better able to concentrate when in class (Lefevre et al, 2013). In a different school he could just as easily have been treated as a truant and put into an isolation wing in the school as a form of punishment (more on this in Chapter 4).

Bakker and Amsing (2009) write on the history of education, and suggest that cultural influences are central to the ways in which we understand and treat children. In an article with a focus on childhood in the Netherlands, they draw upon medical and school-based data spanning the 1900s to 1970s to show that there have always been hyperactive children who lack focus. The authors are also at pains to point out that these children were not previously medicated and that, while poor focus and hyperactivity is nothing new, it is our treatment of children who present in this way that has so vastly changed.

For example, the pharmacological development of drugs to alter the behaviour of children, particularly the introduction of Ritalin or methylphenidate in 1970, has completely altered the treatment of hyperactive and easily-distracted children. Ritalin is a product of today's highly medicalised society. Before this drug came into existence, teachers and parents supported 'neurasthenic' or 'nervous' children differently, and their treatments were discussed by educationists, psychiatrists and psychologists. Experts did recognise that these children were at risk of getting into trouble, but teachers were encouraged to use pedagogical tact and to operate in a calm and supportive manner instead of routinely administering a drug. It seems then that the shift towards using pharmaceuticals does not have to be inevitable.

In fact, drug treatments are far from perfect. The first major trial into the effects of Ritalin on behaviour was conducted by Leon Eisenberg and Keith Conners, then of Johns Hopkins University in Baltimore (Eisenberg and Conners, 1963). The results of the trial were viewed as a triumph for Ritalin. But a close analysis reveals a more complex picture. Set in a residential facility, the trial did not study schoolchildren but hospitalised children. This suggested that the behaviour being assessed was relatively severe. The researchers also noted that, while the behaviour of the subjects improved, there were serious side effects in

70 per cent of the children. These side effects were worrying enough to place the double-blind nature of the trial at risk. Finally, Eisenberg and Conners' conclusion was not a blanket endorsement of the drug but a recommendation for more research. Later in life, both men expressed the view that ADHD was over-diagnosed and Ritalin was overprescribed.

Children are expected to sit still and concentrate for extended periods of time, and those who lack focus and seem hyperactive may be given a diagnosis of ADHD and medicated with Ritalin to enhance capacity to focus and concentrate. It is claimed that this allows children to blend in with the formal education system. Bakker and Amsing (2009) also argue that medication takes the pressure off parents and teachers because they do not want to be blamed for bad practices, and nor do children want to be held responsible for their inability to focus. In addition, the study of psychiatric disorders has traditionally been underpinned by an *a priori* assumption that individuals who meet criteria for a given disorder are comparable, yet when we explore differences across countries, we can see that they are not.

Culture and ADHD and oppositional defiant disorder

Russell et al (2013) examined self-reporting of ADHD and ASD among parents of children in the UK Millennium Cohort Study. Their findings suggest that the proportion of children recognised with ADHD by doctors in the UK is lower than the proportion of children diagnosed in the US (1.4 per cent in this UK estimate recorded in 2013 as opposed to 6.3 per cent recorded in the closest US comparator). They suggest that this difference in clinical practice is due to differing cultural factors in consideration of the ADHD label. Their study underlines the need to establish whether trends are underpinned by increasing risk or merely reflect changes in diagnostic practice. Other studies have also highlighted interesting environmental links. For example, de Zeeuw et al (2015, p 406) found the heritability of oppositional defiant disorder (ODD) and ADHD behaviour was lower for children in different classrooms compared to children who were sharing a classroom, suggesting that different behaviour is elicited within different classroom environments. This American-based study concluded that '*apparently, teachers, the classroom and/or peers are important environmental factors that influence the expression of ODD and ADHD behaviour in primary school*' (de Zeeuw et al, 2015, p 406).

A critique

Whatever the diagnostic preference and outcome, there is still much debate within the fields of psychiatry and psychology about the significance of particular influences in shaping which children will and will not develop underlying mental health difficulties. For now, let us return to the subject of childhood anxiety and to the starting point for this chapter, in which we discussed a decline in symptoms among some children when the pandemic prevented them from attending school.

Defining anxiety

A review of the most influential literature on anxiety tends to treat it as learned behaviour. Research by Cartwright-Hatton et al (2018) at the University of Sussex indicates that mental health disorders run in families, and that environmental factors are significant in the likelihood of children going on to experience emotional challenges. As a result of these findings, her team have developed a supportive intervention programme for parents so that they can go on to parent differently (after all, if anxiety is learned then they may also have been raised by an anxious parent).

To date, the programme has had positive results, and has been successful in reducing risks of heightened anxiety in children while also improving the mental health and welfare of parents. So perhaps it was the case that some children with pre-existing anxiety experienced respite while living at home with their families during lockdown because they generally feel more worried or overwhelmed when they are moving around in their wider community. These pandemic-based findings are worth further investigation. Some families may have enjoyed the downtime that was imposed on them and benefitted from being given societal permission to retreat into their immediate family group. Or perhaps some parents might have felt happier and more relaxed knowing that their children were physically close by and safe from wider societal influences.

The findings suggest that there is value in completing further investigation into the ways in which children and young people might thrive with small alterations to their daily routines. It also indicates that there are particular associations between childhood and psychiatric disorders which our standardised treatment of childhood exacerbates. The standards by which we measure and think about our children's lives are driven by societal norms and values, and it is currently the norm for individual family members to spend the majority of their day away from each other in separate localities.

As suggested earlier in this chapter, if we are to properly understand and show empathy for children who are experiencing difficulties and are suffering emotionally, then there is also value in stepping back from established ideas about mental health and the normative treatment programmes associated with particular conditions to examine where they came from and what informs them. In the light of this it is also useful for us to take a critical look at the interpretation and application of statistics on the subject of childhood.

Childhood in crisis?

We opened this chapter with a premise that today's children and young people are experiencing an unprecedented mental health crisis. A quick trawl through our newspapers and the internet reveals headlines reporting that children and young people growing up in contemporary Britain are more anxious and worried than they have ever been. While reading this chapter I suggest that you explore this claim and take a moment at some point to put the terms 'news', 'children' and 'mental health' into a search engine to see the type of responses revealed by your interest in this area. I did likewise and found that most of the articles focused on negative aspects of childhood. The following, taken from the *Daily Telegraph*, is representative of what my search revealed: '*Almost half of young adults at clinical risk of mental health disorders in "profound crisis" study shows*' (Rigby, 2021). This article was based on a study by Imperial College London, by Dewa et al (2021), which also reported that 30 per cent of young people had poor mental health in the first Covid-19 lockdown. Other studies reported that more children are anxious and depressed than ever, and that British children are some of the unhappiest in the developed world. The mental health focused charity Young Minds reports similarly unsettling statistics, stating that the prevalence of 5–15 year olds experiencing emotional disorders (including anxiety and depression) has increased by 48 per cent – from 3.9 per cent in 2004 to 5.8 per cent in 2017 (NHS Digital, 2021).

Reflections on cultural norms

It is very apparent that there is continual and repetitive coverage, both in the media and among expert bodies, on the subject of poor mental health among the young. This continual and unwavering coverage of childhood as a difficult and traumatic time is now commonplace. On the one hand, having licence to speak freely about one's emotions is likely to be quite a freeing exercise and, done well, could further a person's capacity to reflect upon the formative experiences that are influencing them and help them to develop coping strategies. Alternatively, if young people and their families merely absorb coverage found in non-profit-based studies and media-fuelled messages, then they might in turn assume that it is inevitable that poor mental health is on the rise. The dominant discourse renders children, young people and their families powerless. We are in danger of creating a culture that is unwittingly exacerbating distress in its younger members. Yet contemporary reporting on mental health issues is not only open to very broad interpretation but is only substantiated by very poorly analysed data. This approach to our understanding of mental health first arose in 2007.

2007: a change takes place

Today, references to anxiety, ADHD and depression are part of our everyday discussion of childhood experience. Those who enter formal mental health services will expect to receive a diagnosis of anxiety, depression or ADHD.

Yet our current ideas about children's mental health are not fixed. It's possible that we could trace our current 'catastrophe'-based understanding of children's mental health back to a report published by UNICEF in 2007 titled *Child Poverty in Perspective: An Overview of Child Well-being in Rich Countries. A Comprehensive Assessment of the Lives and Well-being of Children and Adolescents in the Economically Advanced Nations* (UNICEF, 2007). At the time, the findings received extensive publicity in the British media because one of its findings placed the UK's children at the bottom of the league table of rich nations in relation to emotional well-being and 'happiness'. All of the national papers reported on the unhappiness of British children and questions were asked at government level about where we were going wrong, and why it was that so many other countries were doing so much better than us? The Office for the Children's Commissioner offered funding for academics to look into ways to enhance the happiness of children (the report I worked on being one of them).

There were a number of responses to the report, most of which fell in line with the conclusion from the UNICEF study. Media coverage did not include key details, such as whether children from different cultural backgrounds understood phrases such as happiness, sadness and well-being differently, or whether the same number of children had taken part in the study within each jurisdiction. Two child-focused academics, Ginny Morrow and Berry Mayall, were concerned and decided to analyse the report in detail. In a seminal paper published in 2009, they not only discredited UNICEF's claims but raised concern about the coverage of UNICEF's concluding remarks in the British press. Morrow and Mayall (2009) documented the way in which different media broadcasters repeatedly returned to the subject of British children's unhappiness year after year.

The need for thorough analysis

In their paper Morrow and Mayall (2009) ask why one report was taken as fact and reported so widely without rigorous analysis of the ways in which the data had been used and applied. They point out that the numbers of children involved in the study differed from country to country. Might British children have different expectations of normative values and quality of life experiences than children growing up elsewhere? Anomalies such as these, even when thoroughly explored, make it difficult for cross-country comparisons to be accurately made. Morrow and Mayall are not alone in having drawn quite different conclusions from UNICEF's findings. Ansell et al (2007) also state that *'given the limitations of the report… it is worrying that its findings have been accepted unproblematically by much of the UK media and many policy makers'* (Ansell et al, 2007, p 29).

Perhaps then the speed with which the media ran with such a negative portrayal of British children's lives is the most useful and revealing outcome of the report. Instead of focusing on the apparent unhappiness of children and young people, might our time be better spent examining why the story has been so frequently referred to on different platforms in the press?

Other ways to think about mental health

There are other studies that have also been tracking the state of young people's mental health, and which refer to a different set of findings. In 2018, the British government published its most recent mental health survey of children and young people (Sadler et al, 2018). Despite a widespread perception that children and young people today are more troubled than previous generations, the findings revealed that there has only been a slight increase over time in the prevalence of reported mental distress from 9.7 per cent of children in 1999 to 10.1 per cent in 2004, to 11.2 per cent in 2017. The report also highlighted a change in the type of diagnosis being offered to children, which is age dependent; younger children are more likely to be given a hyperactivity-related diagnosis and older children a low-mood-related diagnosis.

The report also found that low levels of social support are also of significance. School exclusions are more common in children who present with mental health issues; for example, the study found that one boy in ten with a formal diagnosis had been excluded from school. Among the children in the survey, one in 50 (2 per cent) 15 to 19 year olds were taking medication for a mental health related problem (Sadler et al, 2018).

Other studies have reported similar findings. The NHS long-term plan published in 2019 summed up issues affecting children and young people by highlighting that mental health problems often develop early in childhood. On the face of it, it seems that diagnosable mental health conditions are not significantly on the rise but that some groups of children are more likely to receive a formal diagnosis than others.

There is also further room for optimism. Other studies, such as the *Children's Worlds National Report* (Rees and Bradshaw, 2020), which has been collating information about children around the world since 2014, also include more positive data. In their study of British children, one-third of all ten year olds who were asked about their psychological well-being said it was very positive, and a further 61.6 per cent said it was positive most of the time. In the same survey, 63.7 per cent of children asked liked the way they are and a further 24.5 per cent mainly liked the way they are (Rees and Bradshaw, 2020).

Conclusion

The purpose of this chapter is to show that our mental health and how we understand it does not exist in a vacuum. Despite the existence of contradictory evidence, there is a generally held perception across our society, one perpetuated by the media, that poor mental health is on the increase among our children and young people. There is also an emerging language of distress associated with children's expression of challenging feelings and trauma. Gone are the days when we simply referred to feeling sad and upset. Instead, reference is routinely made to feelings of anxiety, depression and our poor mental health, which is partly fuelled by social media and the mainstream media. I suggest that the current practice of adopting such language runs the risk of pathologising the normal ups and downs of everyday experience. Our current approach to mental health also makes it harder to distinguish between those who really are in dire need of support and those who are requesting specialist care based on self-diagnosis.

We are experiencing a saturation in need for mental health support for a variety of reasons, some of which were outlined in Chapter 1. With those previous points in mind, it would be easy to place the blame on children, teenagers and their families, but to do so would be a grave injustice. Instead, we could explore injustices within wider society, the impact of our societal narrowing of acceptable forms of childhood, and a media and social media fuelled assumption that poor mental health is on the rise. As suggested in the previous chapter, it is time to develop a new way of talking about and supporting people's mental health needs.

References

Ansell, N, Barker, J and Smith F (2007) UNICEF 'Child Poverty in Perspective' Report: A View from the UK. *Children's Geographies*, 5(3): 325–30.

Bakker, N and Amsing, H (2009) The Discovery of Inequality: Educational Research in the Netherlands in the 1950s. ISCHE 31 Conference: Educating the People, Utrecht, the Netherlands.

Barclay, K, Crozier-De Rosa, S and Stearns, P (eds) (2020) *Sources for the History of Emotions: A Guide*. Oxford: Routledge.

Boyle, A (2011) Parenting Aggravation and Autism Spectrum Disorders: 2007 National Survey of Children's Health. *Disability and Health Journal*, 4(3): 143–52.

Cartwright-Hatton, S, Ewing, D, Dash, S, Hughes, Z, Thompson, E, Hazell, C, Field, A and Startup, H (2018) Preventing Family Transmission of Anxiety: Feasibility RCT of a Brief Intervention for Parents. *British Journal of Clinical Psychology*, 57(3): 351–66.

Creswell, C, Waite, P and Hudson, J (2020) Practitioner Review: Anxiety Disorders in Children and Young People— Assessment and Treatment. *Journal of Child Psychology and Psychiatry*, 61(6): 628–43.

Dewa, L et al (2021) CCopeY: A Mixed-Methods Co-produced Study on the Mental Health Status and Coping Strategies of Young People during COVID-19 UK Lockdown in the UK. *Journal of Adolescent Health*, 68(4): 666–75.

Eisenberg, L and Conners, C (1963) The Effects of Methylphenidate on Symptomatology and Learning in Disturbed Children. *American Journal of Psychiatry*, 120: 458–64.

Goldenberg, M (2006) On Evidence and Evidence-Based Medicine: Lessons from the Philosophy of Science. *Social Science & Medicine*, 62(11): 2621–32.

Goody, J (1977) *The Domestication of the Savage Mind*. Cambridge: Cambridge University Press.

Hartley, L (1953) *The Go-Between*. London: Hamish Hamilton (Penguin).

Kleinman, A (1988) *The Illness Narrative: Suffering, Healing and the Human Condition*. New York: Basic Books.

Lambert, H (2006) Accounting for EBM: Notions of Evidence in Medicine. *Social Science & Medicine*, 62(11): 2633–45.

Lefevre, M, Burr, R, Boddy, J and Rosenthal, R (2013) *Feeling Safe, Keeping Safe: Good Practice in Safeguarding and Child Protection in Secondary Schools*. London: Office of the Children's Commissioner for England.

Madjar, N et al (2019) Childhood Methylphenidate Adherence as a Predictor of Antidepressants Use During Adolescence. *European Child & Adolescent Psychiatry*, 28: 1365–73.

McCrory, E J, Gerrin, M I and Viding, E (2017) Annual Research Review: Childhood Maltreatment, Latent Vulnerability and the Shift to Preventative Psychiatry – the Contribution of Functional Brain Imaging. *Journal of Child Psychology and Psychiatry*, 58(4): 338–57.

Moncrieff, J and Timimi, S (2013) The Social and Cultural Construction of Psychiatric Knowledge: An Analysis of NICE Guidelines on Depression and ADHD. *Anthropology and Medicine*, 20: 59–71.

Morrow, V and Mayall, B (2009) What Is Wrong with Children's Well-being in the UK? Questions of Meaning and Measurement. *Journal of Social Welfare & Family Law*, 31(3): 217–29.

NHS Digital (2021) *Mental Health of Children and Young People in England 2021*. [online] Available at: https://digital.nhs.uk/data-and-information/publications/statistical/mental-health-of-children-and-young-people-in-england/2021-follow-up-to-the-2017-survey (accessed 18 June 2022).

Oosterhoff, B, Palmer, C A, Wilson, J and Shook, N (2020) Adolescents' Motivations to Engage in Social Distancing During the COVID-19 Pandemic: Associations with Mental and Social Health. *Journal of Adolescent Health*, 67(2): 179–85.

Rees, G and Bradshaw, J (2020) *Children's Worlds National Report: England*, July 2020. York: SPRU.

Rigby, J (2021) Almost Half of Young Adults at Clinical Risk of Mental Health Disorders in 'Profound Crisis' Study. *Daily Telegraph*, 15 March.

Russell, G, Rodgers, L, Ford, T and Ukoumunne, O (2013) Prevalence of Parent-Reported ASD & ADHD in the UK: Findings from the Millennium Cohort Study. *Journal of Autism & Developmental Disorders*, 44(1): 31–40.

Sadler, K, Vizard, T, Ford, T, Goodman, A, Goodman, R and McManus, S (2018) *Mental Health of Children and Young People in England, 2017: Trends and Characteristics*. Leeds: NHS Digital.

UNICEF (2007) *Child Poverty in Perspective: An Overview of Child Well-being in Rich Countries. A Comprehensive Assessment of the Lives and Well-being of Children and Adolescents in the Economically Advanced Nations*. Report Card 7. Florence: UNICEF Innocenti Research Centre.

de Zeeuw, E, van Beijsterveldt, C, Lubke, G, Glasner, T and Boomsma, D (2015) Childhood ODD and ADHD Behavior: The Effect of Classroom Sharing, Gender, Teacher Gender and Their Interactions. *Behavior Genetics*, 45(4): 394–408.

4 Children and young people, the school system and reactionary practice

Baroness Butler-Sloss: 'the child is a person not an object of concern'.

Munro (2011)

In this chapter, we will focus solely on the significance of education during the formative years and discuss the ways that schooling influences and shapes children's behaviour. The majority of children growing up in the UK spend a significant amount of their waking day away from home and in educational settings. As we show here, the school experience is a mixed one; while some children enjoy and thrive during their school years, others will have a varied, or entirely negative, response to that period in their lives. In Chapter 3, we briefly touched on this variability when examining children's feelings about staying at home during the height of the pandemic. To recap: research completed during the pandemic suggests that secondary school aged children who normally experienced anxiety and depression tended to enjoy lockdown time with their families, and felt more emotionally stable than they did when in school. In contrast, children of primary school age were generally more likely to miss going to school. This finding reflects longstanding concerns, raised by the Children's Commissioner for England (OCC), about the ways that secondary schools generally engage with pupils. OCC evidence shows that we do a good job of supporting children's emotional well-being while they are at primary school, but once children are at secondary school they tend to get lost within the system, and acts of defiance are more likely to be treated punitively rather than as indicators of unrest or distress (Tillson and Oxley, 2020).

Some of the challenges facing secondary schools are structural. Secondary schools are large institutions, and when children join at age 11, they will be doing so from a pool of much smaller school settings. It is also easier to spot challenges facing children in small school settings, and, as I showed in Chapter 2 when we discussed developmental stages, we tend to consider distress in younger children through a protective lens. In the teenage years, when young people are also preparing for greater independence, their feelings of upset will manifest themselves differently. Some children will carry challenging life events and internalise them, perhaps not recognising them for what they are until they are older and feel more able to do so. Others will look to their peers for help and, having been let down by adults in their lives, will be less willing or able to open up to caring adults in the secondary school setting, and may instead show their distress by being defiant (as shown in the section on the experience of Sid later in this chapter).

How should we offer support?

None of these reactions are easy for schools and teachers to manage but, as we show in this chapter, there are significant differences in how individual schools are choosing to respond to young people in their care. With this last point in mind, it is useful for all professionals working with young people to have psycho-social insight into why children act out in the way that they do. At present, teacher training does not cover this area in enough detail.

Recognising that some secondary school environments are becoming more punitive in response to misbehaviour, the OCC made funding available for researchers to visit secondary schools that scored high in Ofsted reports on emotional well-being. The aim was to determine the conditioning factors and then disseminate the findings across the country for other schools to learn from. This chapter is partly informed by the research that my colleagues and I at the University of Sussex subsequently carried out on this subject for the OCC (Lefevre et al, 2013). It also draws upon follow-on fieldwork that I then completed that was inspired by what I learnt while working on the OCC project.

While completing fieldwork for the project, I was struck by how adult-led young people's support services are, and how rarely children and young people are asked to take the lead on anything. If they reveal (and many probably choose not to) that they are struggling emotionally, then the standard process is for adults to offer support and come up with solutions. Parents might get involved and take a child to their GP. A referral might be made to CAMHS (Child and Adolescent Mental Health Services) where children are assessed to see if they meet the threshold for a mental health diagnosis (this being the gateway to services).

Follow-up research

After the OCC study came to an end, I decided to return to my origins as an anthropologist to complete the longitudinal body of fieldwork in a local secondary school that informs this book. My purpose was to work with a group of children on their terms and, following their guidance, see if we could jointly develop long-term strategies that they might use across the life-course to apply independently to various life challenges without the need for on-going adult support. I also decided to adopt a similarly longitudinal fieldwork approach to the one that I had previously successfully employed while working with children in Vietnam. Therefore, I decided to focus the first six months of the study on simply building trusting relationships with the children that I met, so that our discussions were open and genuine!

Secondary school experiences are important for everyone

Chapters 5 and 6 will focus on the practical techniques that emerged out of this process. In this chapter, we will examine some of the ways that secondary schools respond to young people in their care. Whether you have an interest in early years, primary-aged children or older children, this chapter is relevant because the vast majority of children grow and take part in the secondary school process, and as I show next, it is important that we properly prepare them for that stage in their lives.

Schooling

It used to be that a child did not have to formally enter school until the term that they turned five years of age. Today, children are encouraged to enter pre-school settings, where there is also an expectation that they will begin to work through the national government-led early-years curriculum. By the time they turn four years of age, all children in the UK are expected to go to school or to be home schooled with adherence to the same age-specific national curriculum. During their time in the formal education system, children are required to take nationally standardised tests designed to measure their cognitive abilities against those of their peers. It is expected that at 16 years old they will all take nationally regulated qualifications in the form of GCSEs. Then, once they have left secondary school, all young people are legally required to be in some form of full-time education until they are 18 years old.

It is not only children who are measured and compared at school. Schools are pitched against each other and measured for academic outcome and the extent to which they address children's overall development, emotional well-being and mental health. At this point in time our education system is overwhelmingly results led. This creates both advantages and disadvantages. In principle, it creates a system which maximises the opportunity for all children to experience a similar standard of education and therefore a similar start in life. From a central government perspective, it is helpful to measure and compare how the nation's population is doing. We need a skilled workforce to advance the state and to keep up with the progress of other countries.

But there is a downside to our current focus on testing our children. In short, we are creating a comparison culture, which is also in turn narrowing our understanding of what makes for an acceptable and successful childhood. For children who do not 'fit' this societal yardstick of acceptability, this focus on a particular type of education is creating real difficulties. Instead of stepping back from and critiquing contemporary treatment of our children, we are increasingly problematising the behaviour of individuals. This is of real significance for children who, for whatever reason, are not making the mark in school. Set against standard notions of outcome, the so-called under-achievement of this group limits their life choices, but also has a negative effect on their school's Ofsted rating. It is also creating a culture where it is acceptable for schools to internally exclude the least academically able and even withdraw children who have been labelled as having special needs during the period in which standardised testing is taking place, so as to improve their ranking.

Joined-up thinking

No matter what our specialism, areas of interest and reason for reading this book, we should all embrace a duty of care and talk properly across the professions about the complex needs of children and young people, because a large number of the children who we should be working with are the ones who are seen as failing, who are excluded from school for being disruptive, and who are so often labelled with shoddily prescribed learning disorders such as ADHD and autism. This chapter explores our current support services via the experience of three children, Jack, Beth and Sid, with whom I worked during fieldwork over a four-year period.

Jack's experience of the school system

When I met Jack he was 11 years old. His school notes described him as bright and having autism. Jack was referred to the support group that I was in the process of setting up because he was struggling to make friends, and was showing his frustration by being disruptive in class. His parents seemed to be concerned and were phoning the school on a weekly basis to say how worried they were about Jack's isolation and lack of confidence.

The small group setting

Jack thrived in the small group setting that we were setting up. We had clear boundaries allowing each person space to talk, and over the next two years Jack came regularly to the sessions. Early on we established a particular structure for the groups, which were made up of no more than seven pupils. As part of the process, each person was given the opportunity to talk about what they had done that they were proud of or pleased about since the group had last met. In Jack's case (as with most of the boys), he initially spoke solely about successful online gaming results. But, over time, he also relaxed enough to start to make jokes with the other boys in his group and to trust them.

Establishing boundaries and a routine

A few months into the sessions, the boys developed the technique of each group member briefly sharing three positive and three difficult experiences that had occurred during the time since we had last met. This method of stimulating discussion emerged naturally out of informal chatter as each group settled into its own tempo, and over time it became the established format for them to start their session in this way. Each group also established that no one could interrupt a person while they were speaking. As a result, they began to intuitively appreciate the value of properly and respectfully listening to each other (this process is set out in detail in the following chapter).

Being respectful and trusting

Establishing an opening routine was key to each group moving on to talk about creating respectful boundaries. We agreed that the group would be a safe and confidential space where each person could speak freely without interruption. My only caveat was that if I detected that a young person was in danger and experiencing significant difficulties, I would need to discuss this with them in confidence and, if necessary, share concerns with members of the school safeguarding team.

For the first few months the boys' discussions were focused on online gaming. If we had been in a formal teaching session this would have been discouraged, but instead I let them talk on the subject for some time because it felt more important to let them be themselves and feel comfortable in the new and unfamiliar space that we were creating. This approach echoes the work of the humanist psychologist Carl Rogers, whose basic tenet was '*unconditional positive regard*' (Rogers, 1951). As the weeks went by and the boys felt more relaxed and trusting of each other, we began to revisit the three positive and difficult experiences that established the opening of each session and incorporate them into their wider lives.

Jack moves away from discussions about gaming

Over the next few months, Jack still talked about gaming but also mentioned examples of ways in which he was beginning to look beyond himself and become involved in thinking about other boys in his tutor group or in the support group: like '*saving a seat for a boy to sit down in the school dining room*', or '*picking someone's bag up when they had dropped it*' – all small but thoughtful things. As he and the other boys settled into the group, he also started to refer to them as his friends.

The small group setup worked really well for Jack. The other boys in the group became increasingly aware that their presence in Jack's mind as friends was important to him, and they went out of their way to be kind to Jack both in our group meetings and more generally during their average school day.

School exclusion units

Six months into our meetups, Jack appeared at the session in an agitated and wired state. His teacher had let him out of the school exclusion wing at my request to come to our group session. This obviously meant that Jack had been in trouble and removed from his classroom. The teacher told me that Jack had 'kicked off' (in other words, been disruptive) in school and so had immediately gone to the unit. '*Why though?*' I asked. The teacher did not seem to know what it was that had upset Jack and did not seem to be interested in the source of his disturbance. Yet, from my experience, it was not like Jack to be so disruptive. He was clearly upset about something.

A year later, long after the event that had led to an internal exclusion, Jack used our session to discuss aspects of his home life. Seemingly out of nowhere he told the group members: '*I do not like it when my dad drags me off my PlayStation by shoving me against the wall.*'

It turned out that this was a regular occurrence, and that Jack's father was volatile and unpredictable. It also seemed that Jack had been living with the ongoing stress of managing his father's unpredictable behaviour on a long-term basis. During the session we listened to Jack, without judgement or comment. Jack held a stone in his hand while he talked (more on this in Chapter 6), and on this occasion his focus was on the weekend and his evident fear. He did not follow the normal process of speaking to three positive and three challenging aspects of his life, and unusually no one asked him to adhere to the standard format. The four other boys in his group simply listened in silence, and no one pointed out when he had gone over the normal time limit. As he drew to a natural end, Jack tried to laugh his experience off. The room fell silent, and after a few minutes one of the other boys quietly put his hand on Jack's arm and said *'Mate, I do not think I would find it funny if my dad did that...'* and in the empathetic silence that followed Jack found the courage to continue. He quietly spoke about his father having dragged him down the corridor, and how he had managed to get away and lock himself in the bathroom until his mum had come home. He went on to say that his father had blamed him for his incapacity to stay in control and that now, as a result of his father having lost his temper, Jack had had his PlayStation confiscated for the next week.

Reflections upon Jack's experiences

In Chapter 2 we explored the long-term effects of living in a home environment where behaviours are unpredictable and inconsistent. We also spent time exploring how such abuses affect our sense of self, and how hard it is for children to open up and feel safe to share abuses of trust. Further into this chapter we examine Jack's experience in relation to the toll that such unkind treatment would have been taking on his physiological, psychological and cognitive development. But for now, let's step back from Jack's experience and think about the way in which his expression of distress was being managed and understood in the school environment.

Crowd control = exclusion

From the school's perspective, Jack was quick to lose his temper, and because this was a regular occurrence it was standard that when he did so he would be taken out of the classroom setting so that other children could get on with their work undisturbed. In a large class, and with limited options available to a teacher, this makes sense. It is what happened next that becomes problematic.

As a result of being ordered out of the classroom Jack now felt targeted and, while he was aware that he had been badly behaved, he was also feeling scared, but was probably also gaining some physical relief from being able to act out the pent-up hurt that had been building up in the aftermath of his father's poor treatment of him.

If he had had a trusted person to confide in, his actions might have been treated as a call for help. But Jack was not spoken to empathetically. Instead, he was chastised and taken to the exclusion unit, where he was made to sit staring at a blank wall with nothing to do but 'think about his actions'. No wonder he felt frustrated, disengaged and increasingly angry with everybody because from his perspective, and in all accuracy, no one was actually listening to or paying attention to the real cause of his outbursts.

Applying labels too readily

Time and time again, teachers told me that Jack could be a delight one on one but having Asperger's/autism was at the root of his behavioural problems. I was told that his parents were worried about him, were concerned about his lack of friends and felt that if he had a group to hang out with in school everything would be alright. None of the teachers were aware, until I was able to share what Jack had shared with the group, that there were problems at home and that Jack was being aggressively disciplined by his father.

Treating children's expressions of distress in isolation

No one was properly joining up the dots on why it was that Jack was losing his temper, answering back and generally being disruptive in class, or doing the same for other children who were also creating disruption within the school setting. There was little regard for the fact that people tend to express their unhappiness overtly and obviously only when they feel relatively safe to do so. No one seemed to have the expertise to apply Bandura's social learning theory to their observations, and ask whose behaviour angry children were replicating when they violently expressed themselves (see Chapter 2). Or whether disciplinary action within the school setting was a form of light relief for neglected children who so crave attention that any style of interaction from an interested adult would do, and would momentarily alleviate some of the distress caused by maltreatment. Or whether children were also becoming withdrawn or getting upset because of underlying learning needs in the form of dyslexia or dyspraxia, which were not being adequately supported.

Some positives

Meanwhile, Jack was building a few friendships with some of the boys in our group. They were starting to see that there was a connection between when Jack 'kicked off' in school and when he had been treated badly at home. He was beginning to get empathy from the boys in the group. He was also making eye contact with members of the group and myself during our sessions. The capacity to make eye contact showed a level of comfort and trust that he had not been capable of at the beginning of his time with us, and obviously enhanced his capacity to communicate in a positive and reciprocal manner with others.

After two years of coming to our group sessions, Jack decided he no longer wanted to come along and, for him, it was timely that he no longer did so. Little had changed at home (this was a person for whom social services were not going to make much difference: low-level neglect does not meet the threshold for social work intervention). Two years in to the group sessions, however, he was relaxed with the group of boys he had met in our sessions and was happy to chat with me. He would make jokes, take the time to see how people were, and would often make a point of arriving a bit earlier than the other boys in the group to have a catch-up. He had also learned through our group work about the origins of anger, and that it was not his fault that his father could not control his temper. More on this and other methods that we developed in Chapters 5 and 6.

Jack viewed through a limited lens of disability

By this point, I would have been hard pressed to only understand Jack's behaviour through a lens of autism and leave it at that. When we first started working together, I might have described him as lonely and a little bit socially clunky and unsure of himself, but also as thoughtful and eager to fit in, and very keen to make friends and connections with other people within the school community. Knowing what I did, I would also have described him as being deeply wary of adults whom he did not know, and as having a complicated relationship with his dad, who on good days could be very attentive and funny, but on bad days would be frightening to be around. With this in mind I would challenge a *singular* label of autism, for reasons outlined below.

Whenever Jack expressed unrest, autism was seen to be at the root of the problem, and so his upset was taken at face value. This meant that few professionals dug any deeper to ask whether there was anything in particular that was triggering his disruptive behaviour. His parents came across as professional and middle class, and their interest in how he fitted in during the school day was taken to mean that they were also caring parents. They also fitted the profile of parents who push for their child to be diagnosed and prescribed with a condition. In their case, the diagnosis was distracting because it resulted in important questions about child welfare going unasked. It distracted us from properly finding out what was actually going on in Jack's life.

Entering formal services

From a social work perspective, if Jack had been referred by his school to social services, he would have had minimal social work involvement. He may have been treated as a child in need. A social worker might have raised concerns with the parents, and his father might well have expressed denial that anything untoward was happening at home. Jack's professional and middle-class parents might also have raised a complaint against social services if an insightful social worker had raised concerns about domestic abuse. Alternatively, they might have expressed some regret, and a positive shift might have occurred in the way that the family communicated with and treated each other. The parents might have been encouraged to enrol on a parenting course and in time learned that Jack would be far happier if he were to be given clear expectations about when the PlayStation was to be used, and positive reinforcements for adhering to family rules.

Child-centred work in school

Rather than escalating a need for Jack to be labelled and diagnosed, our work together showed that some simple and cost-effective techniques introduced into the school day could make a difference. In essence, Jack needed a little bit of time outside the formal classroom setting in a caring environment, and not in an isolation booth. Once school were aware of issues at home, they changed tactic and sent Jack to the soft seating area in the library to calm down. They also saw that he needed to establish a trusting relationship with an adult in a setting that he was already familiar with. And in time, Jack developed that type of relationship with his year tutor.

He also benefitted from being a member of the support group, and of hearing other boys validate that his father was in the wrong. This was invaluable. It legitimised how Jack was feeling and showed him that it was not alright for him to be treated by his father in the way that he was. It also allowed school to understand that there were reasons for Jack acting out (again) and that there was a pattern to his distress. Jack was far more likely to be volatile on Fridays and Mondays: Fridays because he was preparing for the uncertainty of the weekend ahead, and Mondays because it was safe for him to let off steam in school.

The year after we started working together, Jack was given a place on the school council and became his tutor group representative. This role gave Jack the opportunity to communicate on wider school issues with other people in his tutor group and it gave him a positive role within the wider school community.

Institutions and standardised forms of identity

Jack, and other young people like him who are struggling to conform to our society's expectations of them, seem to come particularly unstuck when faced with the formal constraints of our education system. Both Irving Goffman's work on institutions and Michel Foucault's work on power within organisations (in his case prisons) is relevant here. Both Goffman (1961) and Foucault (1977) provided new ways of thinking about and questioning the everyday rules and regulations that we have grown up with, and which are so ingrained in our sense of normality. Foucault would argue that many of the everyday rules and regulations that inform our lives have been set up to control and limit opportunity. In his examination of *Discipline and Punishment* he argued that '*the function of all institutions is very similar and the power to punish is not essentially different from that of curing or educating*' (Foucault, 1977, p 303).

Goffman's seminal work on asylums goes further and highlights that we are all at risk of being so controlled by the rules of institutions that we either work for or are placed in that we end up losing a personal sense of right and wrong. Instead we take the route of least resistance by conforming in a way that the institutions expect from us. In his research, he looked at life inside institutions and made a distinction between the initial effects of institutionalisation on the inmate's previous social relationships, the ways of adapting once in the institution, and the role of the staff in presenting to the inmate the facts of his or her situation. Goffman found that the most important factor in forming a mental-hospital patient is the institution, not the illness, and that the patient's reactions and adjustments are similar to those of inmates in other types of institutions as well. There are key parallels to be made with the British education system.

Internal exclusion units

The introduction of internal exclusion units into British secondary schools is a very good example of this. Internal exclusion units were only introduced into secondary schools during the mid-1990s in response to a central government expectation that all schools would record the number of children being excluded from school for disruptive behaviour.

By introducing internal exclusion units, schools were able to continue to exert control over children without formally recording their absence. In this way, exclusions could be hidden from central government control and schools did not need to disclose the number of times that they felt the need to discipline children who had broken school rules.

There is a growing concern about the use of exclusion units and growing momentum from a human rights perspective to challenge the methods adopted in such places.

Exclusion units vary in quality. In some schools, children are made to sit for days in isolation booths and to stare at a blank wall. While I was a researcher working on a project for the Office for the Children's Commissioner on emotional well-being in schools, I asked to see the exclusion unit in one secondary school where this practice was going on, and was told that I could not gain access but that it was right that pupils stare at a blank wall because this gives them time to think about their actions.

Yet there did not seem to be any clear guidelines about who was or was not eligible to be sent to the exclusion unit, or any rules laid down about how long an exclusion should last for. I concluded that inclusion in the unit had been set using an arbitrary set of guidelines, and that some children were far more likely than others to be placed in such units. The exclusion units are hidden places within the school, where abuses of power can easily occur without any properly accountable avenue for recourse by pupils, parents or professionals. In March 2018 at the National Education Union meeting in Brighton, a motion was introduced which stated that:

> The increasing use of detention, isolation and exclusion, often talked of as being 'zero-tolerance' approaches, usually mean ignoring the varied difficulties children have, in favour of punishment. We believe that, above all else, children need support, respect and love.

A report by a *Guardian* analysis (Perrandin and McIntyre, 2018) found that 45 schools in England excluded at least 20 per cent of their pupils in the last academic year. The Outwood Grange Academies Trust – which runs 30 schools across Yorkshire, the Humber and the East Midlands – ran nine out of the 45 schools. Outwood Academy Ormesby in Middlesbrough topped the list, with 41 per cent of its pupils receiving at least one suspension in the last academic year. Parents with children at schools in the Trust raised concerns that, as well as the high levels of exclusions, many schools were also using 'consequences rooms' – small booths in which a child sits alone and in silence for hours on end as punishment for breaking school rules. The booths have been described as 'internal exclusions' and parents called on academy trusts to release information on the number of hours of education children were missing while in the booths.

However, these types of exclusion units have now become so mainstreamed that they are becoming standard forms of intervention across the school sector. The locking up of children in isolation booths for days at a time has become normal and, in some schools, students are repeatedly put in isolation for minor misdemeanours.

Yet schools do have a choice about how they choose to control and manage the behaviour of young people, and there is some really creative work going on in some secondary schools. If a child is engaged, is listened to and has a safe and supportive space in which to calm themselves down, they will feel able to re-join their class without feelings of shame and inadequacy.

Might there be links between distress among boys and girls and the use of isolation units? How do they affect the wider school population and not just the children forced into them?

Room for optimism

In 2013 when I was part of the Children's Commissioner England funded research team, my role was to interview teaching staff and students at secondary schools which Ofsted considered to be offering pupils outstanding emotional support. In every school it was the leadership team that set the agenda and acted as positive role models. The headteachers I interviewed were passionate about understanding the underlying reasons for students acting out, and came up with innovative ways of working and also offered regular training to new staff members. Most of them recognised that schools can be noisy, competitive and overwhelming places for young people who lack confidence.

They also engaged with pupils on the basis that gaining qualifications can be life-changing. Children were given clear expectations, discipline was enforced, but it was done so constructively and was finely tuned to the circumstances of each child. In a school in central London, a headteacher had a photo in her office of every student in the school who was known to be underachieving. She knew each student by name and expected her staff to do likewise. One of her successes was to introduce a student-on-student mentoring programme and regularly invite adults from similar backgrounds into the school to give inspirational talks. In another school, the head had set aside a downtime room with soft seating where students could go, not as a form of punishment but because it was recognised that for some letting off steam was a necessity.

In short, it is possible for schools to create their own culture and choose the extent to which they will be punitive or child centred and supportive. For example, the school attendance officer in the same school was aware of which pupils were likely to turn up at school without having had a decent meal the night before and had a stack of breakfast bars and bananas to hand out. In another case, in one county in the north of England social services and education services had established linked relationships between social workers and schools, so that each school had one named social worker attached to their school as a first point of contact. This had made a positive difference to working relationships and created regular points of contact.

Beth's experience in the school

Initially when I set up the support system in the secondary school, only children who were known to social services were referred to me. In one group I had a 12-year-old girl who was in foster care, and in the year that I knew her she changed family placements twice. The school was her place of secure attachment (Jewell et al, 2019) and teachers repeatedly emphasised this point with her social worker. Beth had a love of animals and her social worker had bought her a hamster, which was also of emotional significance to Beth (Tipper, 2011). The well-being of her hamster played centre stage in our discussions, particularly when she was moving from one family to another. We were able to use discussions about her hamster to great effect because, of course, her descriptions of how the hamster was coping was a mirror to her feelings about moving on. It allowed for safe and open discussion about how she was doing.

Because Beth was known to social workers she was treated with empathy by teachers, yet when her second placement unexpectedly broke down, she had to move schools and without notice. She simply failed to turn up at school the following week and we did not see her again. I cannot imagine how this made Beth feel, and we were not given an opportunity to support her through the school transition process. With a little more thought it would have been possible for the transition to take place over a couple of days and for us to do some work with Beth so that the new school move was not too overwhelming. If the school had had a linked social worker attached to it, as was the case in some of the schools that I worked with for the OCC project, we would have been able to at least organise for Beth to come back into school to say goodbye to her friends. A good ending is important and helps with transitions.

The benefits of a participatory approach

There are a number of studies that add weight to my argument that young people and children benefit from being central to decision making and having their views taken seriously. These ideas are reflected in an evaluation report by the NSPCC, which found that children benefitted most when there was sensitive support offered by an advocate who was acting solely on their behalf (NSPCC, 2021, p 13).

Other studies highlight that it is still common for adults to lead on decision making, and that this adult-led approach is detrimental to the people we work with. In 2010, Ofsted (2011) reported 67 serious case reviews, which indicated that professionals did not see the child frequently enough or did not ask the child about their views and feelings. The same study found that professionals also did not listen to adults who tried to speak on behalf of the child and could provide important information about the child, and in addition parents and carers prevented professionals from seeing and listening to the child. In some cases, professionals also focused too much on the needs of the parents and overlooked the implications for the child.

Cossar et al (2014) have talked to children about their experience of the child protection system. They found that when children were not always well informed by professionals, they often had little choice but to resort to piecing together information to make sense of what was happening by getting information from family members. Most crucially, children also wanted to maintain a sense of control throughout the child protection process and did not want to hand over their worries to a professional to sort out. However, they did want to share their worries with a trusted adult in order to find the best solution for making them safe (Cossar et al, 2014). It seems then that a significant number of children and young people do want to take part in the decisions that affect them and would like to be given the tools and opportunities to do so. But for now the dominant social construction of childhood and the teenage years is one in which a protectionist adult-led intervention style dominates.

The experience of Sid

The final example in this chapter is linked to the experiences of a young boy who had been sexually abused by a family member and was being raised by his mum. He had joined the support group that I was running because he had low morale, and it was hoped that being part of a smaller group in the school would be of benefit to him. He often became quite upset in class and said that he was being bullied. Two years into our time together, he was transferred out of the school because he had turned up with a penknife to protect himself. His friends were really upset and worried about the zero-tolerance policy context that had led to Sid being expelled.

I was left feeling that, given his background, and how well he was responding to our group work and his close friends, things could have been dealt with differently. Might his legitimate fear of being bullied have been addressed alongside any decision about how he should be treated? I later learnt that the school that he had been transferred to was larger and more focused on academic results. As the months rolled by his old friends in the group still spoke from time to time about how Sid was doing, and I was told that he was self-harming and was rarely in school. The school had got rid of a problem student, but the problems for Sid had become larger and more significant. My concerns for Sid are echoed in the recent government report on school exclusions. In 2019, the government-led Timpson review on school exclusions concluded as follows:

> It is clear that there is too much variation in how behaviour is managed, both in the support given to children who need it and the use of sanctions when they mis-behave. Because of this, it is too common to see poor behaviour that goes unchal-lenged or is not tackled effectively. In some cases, these children are at school, and in others they are simply moved out of education, or mainstream education, without being given the opportunity to learn from and improve their conduct. This is in nobody's interests.
>
> (Timpson, 2019, p 109)

Summary

In this chapter, I have made the case that we are struggling to properly listen to and take children and young people's views seriously. I have also highlighted that when children show distress, we are not always trained to see it for what it is, and that our capacity to do so declines as children get older.

In formal settings, such as secondary schools, the real distress that some young people experience is often silenced. No wonder so many are struggling and internalising legit-imate feelings of anger and upset. How tragic, too, that we are so quick to reconfigure their legitimate expressions of emotion as deviant and rooted in psychiatric illness, or deviant and rooted in defiance for the sake of it. It is up to all of us to challenge and alert colleagues and other professionals to examples such as those outlined in this chapter. It is time to highlight the benefits of good practice by drawing upon simple ideas that already exist in some parts of the country and which are outlined here. While it is easy to become demoralised, it only takes one or two people to initiate change.

An inspirational example

One of my heroes is June Jolly, who worked as a social worker and nurse in the 1960s through to the 1980s. Her obituary in the *Guardian* in 2016 (Leach, 2016) recalled that she was not scared to challenge the status quo and at '*each place she worked, she fought to convince the medical professionals – nursing staff, paediatricians, surgeons, anaesthetists and matrons – that listening to children's feelings and helping them understand what was being done to them was as crucial as doing it*'.

We can all do likewise. The following chapters and some of the ideas highlighted in this chapter will show you how.

References

Cossar, J, Brandon, M and Jordan, P (2014) 'You've Got to Trust Her and She's Got to Trust You': Children's Views on Participation in the Child Protection System. *Child & Family Social Work*, 21(1): 103–12.

Foucault, M (1977) *Discipline and Punishment: The Birth of the Prison*. New York: Random House.

Goffman, E (1961) *Asylums: Essays on the Social Situation of Mental Patients and Other Inmates*. New York: Anchor Books.

Jewell, T, Gardner, T, Susi, K, Watchorn, K, Coopey, E, Simic, M, Fonagy, P and Eisler, I (2019) Attachment Measures in Middle Childhood and Adolescence: A Systematic Review of Measurement Properties. *Clinical Psychology Review*, 68: 71–82.

Leach, P (2016) June Jolly Obituary: Pioneering Nurse Who Transformed the Emotional Care of Children in Hospital. *The Guardian*, 2 May. [online] Available at: www.theguardian.com/society/2016/may/02/june-jolly-obituary (accessed 18 June 2022).

Lefevre, M, Burr, R, Boddy J and Rosenthal R (2013) *Good Practice in Safeguarding and Child Protection in Secondary Schools*. London: Office of the Children's Commissioner.

Munro, E (2011) *The Munro Review of Child Protection: Final Report: A Child-Centred System*. Cm 8062. London: Department for Education.

NSPCC (2021) *NSPCC Annual Report 2020/21: Protecting Children Today, Preventing Abuse Tomorrow*. London: NSPCC.

Ofsted (2011) *The Voice of the Child: Learning Lessons from Serious Case Reviews*. Manchester: Ofsted.

Perrandin, F and McIntyre, N (2018) Dozens of Secondary Schools Exclude at Least 20% of Pupils. *The Guardian*, 31 August. [online] Available at: www.theguardian.com/education/2018/aug/31/dozens-of-secondary-schools-exclude-at-least-20-of-pupils (accessed 18 June 2022).

Rogers, C (1951) *Client-Centered Therapy: Its Current Practice, Implications and Theory*. London: Constable and Company Limited.

Tillson, J and Oxley, L (2020) Children's Moral Rights and UK School Exclusions. *Theory and Research in Education*, 18(1): 40–58.

Timpson, E (2019) *Timpson Review of School Exclusion*. CP92. London: Department of Education.

Tipper, B (2011) 'A Dog Who I Know Quite Well': Everyday Relationships Between Children and Animals. *Children's Geographies*, 9(2): 145–65.

5   Working with young children

Today you are you, that is truer than true. There is no one alive who is youer than you.

Dr Seuss

This chapter includes a range of approaches for working with children up to about ten years old, either one on one or as part of a small group. If you have a background in teaching and have been involved in running nurture groups for children, some of the content may already be familiar to you; most of what follows is based on techniques I have developed as a teacher and social worker.

Children's lives are socially constructed

Our understanding of children has long been influenced by a protectionist adult-led framework. But I would like us to approach the content of this chapter on the basis that, given encouragement, most children will voice their real thoughts and feelings if they think that they are going to be properly heard. Experience has shown me that if we are considerate and watchful, we can learn so much about the lives of the children we spend time with. Being mindful, and working empathetically, allows us to avoid making the mistake of thinking we know best for children simply by the fact of having once been children ourselves. This was brought home to me when I was in my mid-twenties and working as a child protection social worker in Dublin, Ireland.

A team meeting with social workers

I arrived at my first team meeting to find people talking and laughing and shouting loudly to make themselves heard. A cup of tea and biscuit were thrust in my hands, and within a minute I had been invited to a team picnic the following week. It was a room of noisy banter, so much so that our enthusiastic and impassioned manager, Oona, had to holler above the chatter to make herself heard. Once the room finally fell quiet, she went on to run through the list of families we were currently working with, sharing ideas with each of us and talking all along about this child and that child as being rather 'bold' or 'very bold'. At that point, I had no idea what it meant to be 'bold' but to my mind it conjured up a child who was cheeky, strong and sometimes bolshie. And I really liked the term and the way it was being used. Oona was using it in such a way that to be 'bold' sounded like a badge of honour and, because of some children's circumstances, a necessary personality trait. Used in this context it was suggestive that children have the right to be strong and able and have capacity for self-determination.

As the meeting drew to a close, I was still none the wiser about its exact meaning. My only certainty was that pretty much every family now allocated to me had one or two bold children! I realised that I was going to have to figure out the term by myself, and I also realised that I had a lot to learn about working in child protection in a cultural setting that was quite different to my own.

During the next few months, I met some bold children, some thoughtful children, and others who were old or young for their years. All along my abiding sense was that even the very youngest child is far more knowing than we might think. If we let down our 'adult as elder statesman' guard and show that we are genuinely interested in a child's perspective, he or she will respond, and we will discover far more about their lives than if we go in with a presumption that we know best. I also learnt the importance of not introducing our own agendas if we are going to develop a positive and meaningful relationship with the children we work with.

Silence and tranquillity

During one of my first sessions with my students, I ask them to sit together with their hands placed in their laps and just enjoy the silence in the room. My goal is to get each of them to a place where they are content to be with each other in silent companionability. In these sessions we discuss the power of silence, its use as a weapon to punish and ignore and freeze people out, and its opposite use as a space to create unconditional warmth and acceptance when embraced in a meditative context. Being able to enjoy silence can be very resting. It can give children space to settle in around us and each other (if in a group) and to feel tranquility.

Advanced Western societies are not very good at silence and sitting with another person in companionship without filling each moment with activity or words. Yet I think that it is in the spaces between speaking that we learn so much more about ourselves and each other. It seems though that, as a society, we are less comfortable than we have ever been with sitting in unoccupied silence. When we walk around in public spaces it is unusual to see anyone just sitting and alone, or with someone else, without also having their phone to hand. Phones definitely have their uses, but just sitting or walking along side by side with a child can be very revealing. Done well I think it is one of the most useful activities you can do.

Creating space to hear children

Creating a comfortable waiting space is such a joyful thing to do. If we move away from being afraid of silence and attempting to fill the moments with chatter, we can also move away from thinking that we know what is likely to be on a child's mind, and what it is that they might like to talk about. Instead, the unexpected can be revealed. This is partly because when children are very young, they have not learnt to filter out and be guarded about what they say and share.

As a child protection social worker, I once worked with Callum, a young boy aged six, who had been referred to social services just before summer break because his teacher was worried about his relationship with his stepfather. Callum and I first met in his school library and it was a disaster. He sat there staring at the floor and did not say a word, except to talk briefly about who was in his family and about his pet dog. While reassuring his mum that we were working with her son and the whole family to hopefully offer productive support, I also asked Callum if I could meet up with him and his dog, and go on a few dog walks together.

Over the next few weeks, we met up about three times and just spent about half an hour going around the fields near his house with his dog trotting alongside us. Walking in that way was ideal; it meant we were together side by side in parallel without having to make eye contact, and as a consequence, almost by accident I learnt so much more about him and his life than I would have done in a formal setting. (For the social workers and carers among you, this type of parallel activity can also work well on a car journey). I learnt about his joys and his fears, the fun he had playing with his friends, but also about his worry about his mum and stepfather's new baby replacing him in his mum's affections; about his sadness that his stepdad had never invited him fishing, and his continual nagging worry that he was not very important to his family any more.

Meanwhile, I also learnt from his mum that she did not think that family life was working for her new partner and her. She had tried to compensate by doing all the parenting, and I was left wondering if she ever shared these worries with her husband. After a couple of weeks, I asked Callum if he would like to sit down with his parents and me over a cup of tea to have a catch-up. I also reassured him that we would be led by him, that what he had previously shared with me had been said in confidence, and that he could choose what to share and what not to share. So, we set up a family meeting during which, to my unexpected delight, there was a seminal moment in which Callum's stepfather showed warm surprise on learning from Callum that he had been guarding a secret wish to join him on fishing trips. It turned out that Callum's stepfather had felt excluded from the relationship between Callum and his mother and had started to resent their closeness, going fishing more frequently to get away from the house. The following weekend, Callum and his stepdad took up fishing together and their bond grew, and my support quickly and happily became superfluous.

Engaging in magical thinking

Young children engage in magical thinking. The developmental psychologist Jean Piaget (1962) observed that a child's capacity to think in this way starts to tail off by the time they are ten years old (or 11 years old if growing up in Asia!). In essence, magical thinking is a child's belief that what they wish or expect can affect what really happens. For example, if a child wants very much for something to happen, and it does, the child believes they caused it to happen. It is an important stage in a child's life, and magical thinking can be very reassuring to a child, but also quite difficult to manage if significant difficulties arise, such as parental divorce or the death of someone they are close to.

It is helpful for us to have some insights into where a child's magical thinking might be taking them so that we can be reassuring and genuinely empathetic. Children really *do* see the world differently to adults; working with them and being mindful of this is important. The most seemingly innocuous moment can be a reminder that children exist on a different plane of reality, as the following example illuminates. One Christmas, when my twin sons were three years old, my mum and I took them to visit Father Christmas. Minutes after the visit, and once the boys had opened their gifts from the grotto, one of them looked close to tears. Seeing that he was about to cry I whisked him onto my lap for a cuddle, at which point he looked up at me with a shocked expression and said, '*I asked Father Christmas for a book... but look... it's a toolkit!*' He was incredulous, not because he was used to getting his own way, but because he was at a point in his development where asking for a book could *only* conjure a book! To our relief, on that occasion, his twin had just opened up his gift of a book (when he would much rather have had a toolkit). With a wink and a grin, my mum and I switched the gifts and explained that it was just a twin confusion and an easy mistake for a very busy Father Christmas to make! Their reaction provides a fantastic example of magical thinking at work. Understanding magical thinking provides another layer of appreciation for why we need to be mindful of how children make sense of everything that goes on in their lives, and how it is that they come to think that it is their fault when they are treated badly.

Do not underestimate children

Very young children are keen observers of the people around them. This may seem like an obvious thing to say, but we can also easily overlook or disregard the impact of our behaviour on very young children, and also underestimate their capacity to absorb and observe daily events. In reality, alongside magical thinking, independent thinking also starts early on. While in other people's homes, on play dates or in conversations with friends, they will be absorbing that a wide range of lifestyle choices exist. Given the opportunity, they will also prefer a safe and relaxed environment, or to put it simply, they will actively gravitate towards people who are more likely to make them feel calm and secure. As my father, who was homeless as a child, once said to me, '*children go to the light*'.

Domestic abuse

Early on in my child protection work, I began working with a family in which Maggie, the mum, was enduring regular beatings at the hand of her husband, Robert. Their daughter Lilli was seven years old, and it was the summer holidays. I was asked to do a routine check-in visit by my manager. Without thinking very much of it, I jumped on my bike, cycled to the other end of a nearby housing estate and into a tidy well-kept cul-de-sac of semi-detached houses. When I arrived, I was answered at the door by Lilli, who had dragged a chair up to reach and turn the latch. We had not met before, but I explained who I was and she let me in. As we walked towards the kitchen, Lilli told me her mum was busy. By this time, I could see that things were obviously not as you might expect, but I did not press Lilli on where her mum was; instead, I praised her on her clever skill at opening the door and wondered out loud if she had also been clever enough to make her own lunch. '*Oh yes*', she replied, '*look I can make a tomato ketchup sandwich*'. '*Yummy*', I said, '*and do you make those often?*' '*Oh yes*', said Lilli, '*every day, I have one for supper and breakfast*'. '*Well, isn't that grand*', I replied, '*you get to eat something you love whenever you want!*' It goes without saying that by this time, I was as concerned about the whereabouts and safety of Lilli's mum as I was about Lilli, and I was very grateful that my manager had had a hunch that we should check up on how Lilli and her parents were doing.

In short, Lilli's mum was in the house, but was lying in bed, feeling very fragile after a recent beating. It was an awful situation; Lilli was doing her best, but her mum was just too worn out and too broken to do anything but be physically present. I phoned my manager and we sat together with Maggie and Lilli, eventually managing to persuade Maggie to leave the family home and move into a women's refuge with her daughter. This was such a brave thing to do because after so much time in isolation with only her husband and daughter, Maggie's self-esteem was at rock bottom. Unfortunately, the move was short-lived. After a week Maggie, who had been so courageous, decided to return home with Lilli. But by this time Lilli did not want to go home.

On the morning that Maggie left the refuge, staff tried to persuade her to stay and said that they doubted her husband Robert could have changed enough during such a short time to no longer hurt her. While it turned out that the staff were right, Maggie was not convinced. Her co-dependence with Robert, and the alcohol dependency they shared, ran deep. Lilli was distraught, and so the staff at the refuge phoned my manager to share their concerns about her and Maggie's safety. They also shared their observation that, while at the refuge, Lilli had sometimes lashed out at her mum: a behaviour, in this case, of survival, in which a child mirrors the behaviour of the dominant parent.

Social learning theory

Their observation echoed observations made by the psychologist Albert Bandura (1977), who developed social learning theory and used a bobo doll to show that nursery-aged children mimic the behaviour of the adults looking after them. The staff at the hostel had also witnessed Maggie asking Lilli to run errands but doing nothing to comfort and nurture her daughter. We might deduce from this that Maggie had a poor attachment with her daughter and was an inadequate parent. But if we couple that observation with trauma-informed practice we could also conclude that the on-going abuse had left Maggie traumatised and unable to show empathy at that point in time.

Capacity for empathy and mentalisation

What happened next indicated to me that, at some point in the near past, Maggie had been able to put herself in her daughter's shoes and show what the psychologist Peter Fonagy (2008) refers to as mentalisation. Simply put, Fonagy describes mentalisation as '*having one's mind in mind*': a capacity that comes with having secure bonds and being able to empathise with another person and imagine the world as they see it.

When I arrived at Lilli's home, she looked both relieved and scared and we sat down together, Lilli, her mum and me. While Maggie indicated that she was determined in her resolve to stay put, I asked Lilli to share what she wanted to do. Lilli told her mum that she wanted to go back to the refuge, that she was scared of her dad hurting her mum, and that she did not want to live like this any more.

She begged her mum to go with her, and then said that she wanted '*to be in a family that is better than this one*'. The likelihood is that if Lilli had spent her entire life with abuse, she would not have been able to speak in this way with such determination, because she would have already learnt either that to do so would bring on a beating or that her needs and feelings would be ignored. On that morning, Lilli showed a level of self-determination, strength of character and a desire to also protect her mother, that was incredible. At the age of seven she was very clear that her life could be better, and she was also able to articulate her needs and felt strong enough in herself to be heard. Her capacity to do so also indicated that, with sensitive and caring support, her mum might also be able to go into recovery and start to reclaim her sense of self, so that she could go back to being the engaged parent she had been in the past. Yet for the time being, until her parents realised the seriousness of the situation, we concluded that foster care would be beneficial for Lilli. Unfortunately, extended family members were scared of Lilli's father, and so Lilli went into care, and very quickly began to thrive within a family who had a daughter of a similar age to her.

The importance of a trusting relationship

With that last point in mind, it is helpful to talk to children about who they trust and the values that person holds which makes them trustworthy. When children attend school their parent or carer needs to list an alternative emergency contact. Even the youngest child can be asked for their thoughts on who that person should be. Likewise, if a child has to go into care, their view on who they are going to live with should be considered and responded to.

Young children need to be in touch with their bodies and create boundaries

Our cultural tendency to think about childhood as a playful and innocent time can put us in the odd position of unintentionally enhancing children's vulnerabilities, because unless children have the vocabulary to speak about their bodies, they will be unable to communicate even the most basic concerns. Yet I have seen the most rational adults resist educating young children about what their body parts are called and which areas of their bodies are private spaces. It seems somewhat prudish and more akin to a wish to slow down the passing of time than anything else.

Baby language for body parts

For example, I once worked with a little girl whose mother proudly told me that she had taught her daughter to refer to her vagina as her 'little flower'. I have also heard little boys talk about their sausage or hose! It is confusing to introduce a baby term for a vagina or penis when a child is young and then switch to the anatomical term once they are older. If we adopt this approach children may, quite correctly, conclude that their vagina or penis is something that should not be spoken of. We forget that very young children do not associate their vagina or penis with sex.

If we use the correct anatomical terms with our children right from the moment they are learning the names of other body parts, we are showing them that there is no shame attached to having a vagina or penis, and we are also giving them the confidence to trust and talk with us about that area of their body using language that everyone understands and can relate to. In the long run, adopting a matter-of-fact approach, whether as teachers, carers, social workers or parents, allows children to do the same. It gives children body confidence that can also provide them with a much stronger and confident sense of body ownership, which in and of itself can act as a protective factor as they start to independently navigate their wider world.

Addressing worries

Our capacity to speak about not only our bodies, but other aspects of who we are, is necessary for a healthy sense of self. Sometimes the focus on childhood as a happy time makes speaking about challenging times more problematic than it could be. It is as natural to feel worried as it is to feel happiness and sadness. The following exercise can be done with children in their home, in their classroom or perhaps in a school assembly.

Showing children why holding our worries in is a hard thing to do

Take a pillowcase, and a whole pile of cushions and some heavy objects, such as large books, and then ask a child to load each object into the pillowcase and as they do so explain that each object is a worry... and that it is normal to have worries, and that everyone will have some from time to time. Try to make the pillowcase pretty heavy, so that when you ask a child to pick it up they have to struggle a bit to raise it off the ground, and then talk about the 'heavy load' that is being created. Then stop for a minute and ask, 'what shall we do?' Whether you are working with one child, perhaps as a social worker, or with a group of children, perhaps in an early-years setting at circle time, you will be trying to get children to think about ways in which they might be able to help the child who is struggling with the worries. Children can be asked to share different types of worries with the group, or one on one if not in a group. You can then invite the child/children to take a worry out of the bag and to share it with someone they can trust. At this point, each child can be asked to say who it is that they trust and why it is that they trust them. Then one by one the 'worries' can be placed around the room. By the end of the activity, children will have learnt that worries are normal and that holding them tight inside ourselves is difficult and can make us feel unhappy. They will also have learnt that when we take a worry and share it we feel lighter, they will have learnt that other people have worries, and finally they will have discussed the character traits of the type of people who they can trust.

Worry dolls

Another, but more private, approach for children to manage their worries comes in the form of miniature dolls. Guatemalan worry dolls provide young children with a creative outlet for expressing their worries. I first discovered them when I had young children of my own but wish that I had known about them previously. They can be such a comfort and I would have liked to have given them to some of the children I worked with in child protection. Each bag comes with six little dolls and instructions for children to whisper a worry to each doll, then pop them back into their worry bag and place the bag under their pillow at night, so that overnight their worries can be relinquished to the dolls.

Sometimes it can be helpful to ask a child to share some of their worries, particularly if there has been a significant event in their life that it would be impossible to fix by morning, or to ever put right. But in such cases, such as the death of a person or a pet the child is close to, the child could be encouraged not to ask the worry doll to bring their pet back to life but rather to ask the worry doll to send the deceased dog love and say that they hope she is happy in dog heaven (or in her new life… or whatever fits your worldview or that of the family or child you are working with).

Whatever the situation, it is our job as professionals to let children know that it is never a child's fault if they have a worry or have had someone be unkind to them, and that we will be open to and listen to them but also respect their right to privacy. Worry dolls can help enhance a child's sense of privacy and autonomy when it comes to managing key moments that they are not quite ready to share or never want to share.

A post-box for worries

Once children have been introduced to the bag of worries, whether it be a school, group, home or holiday camp, a little box for worries can be placed somewhere in a public but relatively private space in the building. The worries can then be written up in private and let go of, with children safe in the knowledge that a trusted and named adult will look at the contents and offer support.

Children can also use worry boxes with family members; the organisation Young Minds has some helpful guidance on how parents or carers can manage children's worries in the context of the home.

While the worry box is often used with younger children, the same method can be just as easily used with teenagers, or teenagers can be encouraged to keep a journal into which they off-load their worries.

Children feel safe with boundaries

While it is important to properly listen to children and respect them, this does not mean that anything goes. In general, a laissez-faire approach in which they have few clear expectations and boundaries does not seem to work well for children. Children who learn that they can stay up late, or pretty much get away with rude and offhand behaviour, tend to be less contented than those who are given clear and supportive expectations linked to positive rewards. Young children can also learn to be empathetic by doing good for, and thinking about, the feelings of others. A 'circle of kindness' group, in which nursery-aged children are encouraged to say something thoughtful about the child sitting on either side of them, can be helpful. In other words, as developed by Martin Seligman (1991) in his work on positive psychology, creating clear boundaries for young children furthers their long-term chance of working towards high-level forms of contentment and happiness. Seligman's approach, which is linked to an authoritative style of caregiving, can be very positive.

While this seems sensible and makes sense in reality, some adults really struggle to say no to children. However, it can get easier to say no while also acknowledging a child's disappointment. I had little appreciation of any of this as a young social worker, and just knew that I wanted to protect children, but in the course of protecting I came to a far better under-standing of what made young children feel safe, as highlighted by the following example of my work with a very bold little boy.

Fin and his four younger siblings were referred to us late on a Friday afternoon. Two of Fin's little sisters had shared some experiences with their schoolteachers that indicated an adult cousin was touching them intimately. The family were already known to the authorities, and it was decided that myself, Jenny – another social worker – and two police officers should get the children and their mum into temporary accommodation while we all worked out what was going on. While our manager organised the accommodation, Jenny and I waited at a local police station with the mum and her five children (ranging in ages from six months to seven years old). Fin was the eldest at seven. We were given a large room with a huge table and chairs to wait in, and Jenny and I immediately got out papers and crayons to do some fun activities with the children. The children meanwhile thought it would be far more fun to run up onto chairs, jump onto the long tabletop and then wobble off, all the while Jenny and I ran from one toddler to the next to prevent them hurting themselves during a fall. It was madness! And Fin was delighted.

Finally, we managed to get the little ones sitting down and drawing fun pictures, but Fin was having none of it. He grabbed all the crayons and refused to distribute them. His little brothers and sisters started shouting and crying, and I told Fin that he had to share. Fin jumped around swearing and cursing at me. And over the top of the mayhem, I shouted *'what do you like most in the whole world?'* *'Planes!'* he said *'Planes?'* I shouted. *'Can you make a paper one? Because I can… and I give you my word that if you share those crayons, I will help you and teach you to make a great plane'.* *'I don't believe you'*, he said. *'Try me'*, I replied.

Fin stopped, warily looked at me and then reluctantly started sharing the crayons. I thanked him, asked him to say sorry to his brothers and sisters (which he also reluctantly did) and then, as promised, he and I made a couple of planes and flew them around the room, and we spoke about different types and coloured some in. That was all. As far as I was concerned there was nothing special about that moment (although I had a lovely time). The family went into their temporary accommodation for the night; we quickly discovered who had been interfering with the girls and, with the wider family, made the girls safe. I thought nothing more of it until my next visit to the family home where the normally bold little boy Fin made a beeline for me. He did so on every subse-quent visit, and each time we took a moment or two to make a plane and have a proper one-on-one chat.

It was the simplest of things, a moment in time that most children think little of and would put little store by. But Fin, the apparently tricky and bold child that he was meant to be, had really enjoyed a moment of one-on-one attention and obviously craved it, and also appreciated being brought under control. He taught me so much about the pain caused by the absence of being seen and being given licence to run wild. He was exactly the type of little boy or girl who needed an older child or adult as their special mentor, whether that be in his school setting or a family link worker visiting his home, or spending one-on-one time with a family member who had the skill and time to follow through and be there for him. In short, Fin showed me the importance of being seen, of being given clear boundaries, of modelling good, kind but firm behaviour and, most importantly, following through and acknowledging and responding positively to a child.

To summarise, young children, given the choice, will opt to be in the company of adults who give them boundaries and follow through, not with material gifts, but with the simple act of giving them their uninterrupted attention. Over the years my thoughts have periodically returned to that little boy, and I hope that someone saw the potential in him and recognised that his bolshie ways were really just a shield designed to protect him from the uncertainties within his family. Fin taught me, better than any textbook ever could, that the young child in a classroom, nursery or perhaps in a wider social gathering who seems a bit challenging and 'bold', as the Irish might say, or 'defiant' as the English might, is the very child that we need to put more energy into encouraging and supporting and *not* labelling and punishing. It was not Fin's fault that he was so unruly. His behaviour reflected his experiences.

Fidgety children and blue-tac

Young children need to be physically active and move around, and some find it particularly challenging, when sitting still in the classroom or talking one on one with an adult, to focus without fiddling or doodling. It is through the act of fiddling, touching and doodling that we learn to process and develop our senses. Kinetic sand and a cornflour water mix are frequently used in early-year settings to help children develop spatial and sensory awareness. Yet once children enter the formal school system there is a gradual shift away from focusing on developing a wide range of senses.

For children who were premature at birth, or who have had developmental delay for other reasons, such as living in an abusive home environment, the shift in expectation towards a more formal approach to learning can be bewildering. If a child then has the misfortune to have a class teacher who expects conformity, one who sticks rigidly to the developmental age-defined constraints of our national curriculum, and who does not appreciate that age is only one indicator of ability, problems can quickly escalate. Under such circumstances the child can be treated as a problem child and not as someone who needs caring support.

In essence, fidgeting can be a symptom of a child with poorly developed spatial awareness, who constantly needs to move to gain feedback from their environment. By the time a child has entered Year 1, the sand and water tray will be pretty much off the education agenda! Yet the need to fiddle and touch can be as strong as ever, and fiddling can also be very calming. However, no child wants to stand out and feel different. So, one way to manage this can be to give a child something they can fiddle with and touch. From experience, the fiddle object needs to be discretely chosen and blend in with a child's surroundings. For example, I have found that this could be a little ball of blue-tac or plasticine popped in their pocket to fiddle with as a calming and grounding strategy. You can even reassure them that '*if anyone asks, you can pretend you just found the ball lying around in a classroom*' and they will be delighted by the rebel-like impression such an explanation might create.

Pebbles

We can get into the minds of children using all sorts of fun games. One of my social work students came up with a very simple but effective way of doing so during her child protection placement. A family she was working with happened to live close to the beach. So rather than sit in the house with them she suggested a walk along the seashore. Everyone enjoyed the fresh air, the mum became relaxed, and while they were sitting down to take a rest my lovely student tried to get everyone to say a little bit about how they would like things to be different. One of the children wanted to have more fun, while the mum wanted to be listened to. On finding a marker pen in her bag, my student got each family member to choose their own pebble and then privately write down their hope on it. Next, she asked each person to talk about their hope and why they had chosen it. Then when they were ready, they all threw their pebbles into the sea. It was light-hearted but touched on important feelings. The same practice could be done using bits of paper or dried-out leaves.

Stand up, wave your arms in the air and sit down!

When young children are given the opportunity to use movement as part of their learning, they thrive. Young children find it difficult to sit down and concentrate for long periods of time. One of the primary school heads I worked with introduced a method to his younger year groups where children sat and worked for 15 minutes and then had a five-minute burst of physical activity. Moving between sitting down and doing some physical activity is a way to support children's capacity to absorb information, whether that be in a classroom or as a professional working with children in a different capacity. There are many ideas and resources available on the internet for primary school teachers, most of which can also be used in other settings. I particularly like the five-minute stand up, stretch arms into a star and then patter feet up and down. Or the classic heads, shoulders, knees and toes, or the pitter patter rain dance of hands on a tabletop. To use these methods regularly is also effective in engaging with the whole child!

Some children find it hard to communicate

Sometimes asking a young child how they feel can be overwhelming for them. Children who find it difficult to express themselves might respond well to cartoon pictures showing a sad face, smiley face or unsure face (resources such as these are widely available on the internet). Other children might find scaling from 0–10 useful. When I worked with Callum and his family, I would check in with Callum how his week, since we last had a dog walk together, had been by asking '*from a scale of 0 to 10 with 10 being fantastically brilliant, and 0 being the worst, how are you feeling?*' This approach of scaling emotions can help us gain insight into a child's feelings about all manner of things, from taking part in an activity to paying a visit to someone, and can be used as a starting point for further discussion or just a way of acknowledging where they are at that moment in time.

Learning about emotions

Children who struggle with reading people's expressions and body language can be helped along with specialist games. There are also some widely available board games such as 'Guess Who?' which help children develop everyday skills of observation. I invented a game called the 'Sherlock Holmes game' with a little boy who found it difficult to distinguish between people. At the time I decided that although he was probably on the autistic spectrum, his interests were so book focused that some of our time together could be better spent observing people and making a game of it. The Sherlock Holmes game was quite simple. On our walks together we would briefly say *'It's time for Sherlock Holmes'* as a person passed nearby, and after the person was out of view and earshot, we would share what we had picked up about them. He would lead the way, and perhaps mention the colour of a coat, the length of their hair and then any discernible facial expression, and then we would move on to chat about something else. All along we were developing the 'power of observation' to highlight that there are many ways to see the world.

Children hear voices

During the course of my work in social work and as a lecturer, I have had a few children and young people confide in me that they are hearing voices. As a society we tend to associate hearing voices with mental illnesses such as schizophrenia. Where a child is able to make that link, perhaps because they have a family member living with a psychiatric condition, it will be very scary for them. And yet, although relatively little research has been done on the subject during childhood, hearing voices can be a normal life stage that children grow out of as they move towards their teenage years and become used to managing their internal thoughts and brain chatter. We still know very little about the extent to which schizophrenia is inherited. Research by Sarah Parry and Filippo Varese (2021) based at Manchester Metropolitan University shows that around 8 per cent of children hear voices at some stage in childhood, with up to 75 per cent having a one-off experience of voice hearing. For many children, then, it seems that hearing voices is a pretty normal part of growing up, and it is our reaction to the child which is key to how they go on to feel about their internal voice. Other academics raise concerns about the more concerning aspect of hearing voices during adolescence (Parry and Varese, 2021). However, it seems that if we help and reassure children and young people, and do not pathologise their experiences, they are more likely to treat the voices as a passing phase. As with other childhood experiences, context and the way in which we talk to and support children is everything.

Kindness tree

Finally, one of our societal shifts, perhaps exacerbated by social media, is for children and young people to be more focused on their individual journey through life. If we are hoping to encourage the kind of higher-level happiness that Seligman (1991) has found to be most valuable, then getting into the habit of doing good deeds creates hope and a sense of purpose, no matter our age. Young children, be it at home, with their carer or social worker, in school or a health or a youth setting, can contribute to a kindness tree.

All it takes is some branches popped into a pot, a pile of tie-on labels and for children to get together on a regular basis to jot down an act of kindness on a label to attach to the tree. The acts of kindness need not be grand. I would encourage the opposite.

Introducing children to meditative practice

The kindness tree provides a starting point for helping young children to become familiar with meditative practice because it can be linked to wider discussions about enjoying nature, growing plants from seed and thinking about what we all need to grow in ourselves to be comfortable with who we are. There are so many avenues you can develop with this theme, depending on your level of involvement with a child or group of children. When I first adopted a tree-themed approach, I took the children I was working with outside to walk in a wood so that they could both let off steam and find the branches that we would use for our kindness tree. Later on, we also chose some cress seeds and children planted them on cotton wool to take home and look after.

Getting used to lying down and feeling relaxed in a group

A really fun and low-cost exercise simply involves getting a group of children to lie on their backs on the ground in a long line. Next, a huge piece of fabric can be shown to the group (you can sew old sheets or fun-coloured fabrics together in a patchwork, or use an old parachute), and with a person at each end children can experience having the fabric simply moved up and down as a wave and ripple over and above their bodies. There are multiple ways to extend and use the motion of fabric in the air. Simply feeling the air generated by the fabric can be relaxing. If it is big enough the fabric can be lowered so that children can sit on the edges of it to create a temporary tent-like structure that they can sit in together. It can also be lowered up and down while children listen to a relaxing story or sing a favourite group song. It can also be used as preparation for deep breathing during meditation to help children to learn how to breathe slowly and deeply in rhythm with the fabric as it is moved over and above them.

Bubble breathing

You can also use bubbles to encourage slow deep breathing by inviting children to see if they can slowly make a big bubble grow. Then they can lie down and imagine that they are a bubble and can float off and away. While doing this, do let children know they are safe in that moment, and they can choose whether to keep their eyes open. This activity could be followed up with some bubble drawings in which children (age dependent) can draw a happy moment.

Trees as a way of learning to ground ourselves

The first practice I introduce my groups to, including teenagers, is the rooted tree. We start by simply asking a child or young person to stand with arms to their side and to imagine that their feet are growing roots that are reaching down deep into the ground. This should take a few minutes... there is no need to rush.

Then with their eyes open or closed (it is their option) they can breathe in deeply to the count of three and out to the count of three, and imagine energy drawing up through the roots, up into their spine and to the top of their head, all the while feeling as if the ground is giving them strength and peace. As their breath comes out, and they imagine their energy rising, they can wave their arms into the air above their heads and stand for a little bit of time being a tree (tap into that magic thinking). Then they can stand still and feel the strength of the ground running through their feet.

Once the approach has been mastered, you can then explain that this is something they can do on their own whenever they feel the need and that, if they are suddenly feeling wobbly or unsure, all they need to do is breathe in and out slowly, stop and feel themselves rooted and strong, with energy rising up into their bodies. Next time you see each other, you could then check in to see if any of you had cause to use the technique! It is a lovely and grounding approach to use, and if a child opts out of waving their arms as branches, it is also a very useful technique that can be used in public without anyone else being any the wiser!

In the next chapter we will build upon some of the techniques discussed here.

References

Bandura, A (1977) *Social Learning Theory*. Hoboken, NJ: Prentice-Hall.

Fonagy, P (2008) *The Mentalization-Focused Approach to Social Development*. London: Routledge.

Parry, S and Varese, F (2021) Whispers, Echoes, Friends and Fears: Forms and Functions of Voice-Hearing in Adolescence. *Child Adolescent Mental Health*, 26(3): 195–203.

Piaget, J (1962) *Play, Dreams, and Imitation in Childhood*. New York: Norton.

Seligman, M (1991) *Learned Optimism*. New York: Alfred Knopf.

6 Working with older children

Oh, how I wish I could shut up like a telescope! I think I could, if only I knew how to begin.

Alice in *Alice in Wonderland* (Carroll, 1865)

As I highlighted in Chapter 1, our societal response to children and young people's mental health is linked to a variety of interconnected factors, including an abstract and heavily romanticised construction of childhood. When childhood is treated as a time of innocence and play without responsibility then the child's role is to be passive, happy and sweet. This expectation leaves little room for any expression of upset, depression or anger, and this, when coupled with a society-wide tendency to pathologise negative experiences, is creating a culturally induced mental health crisis.

This chapter is a response to my concerns and observations, particularly among young people I have worked with in secondary schools and during their time in higher education, and outlines methods and techniques to assist children and young people towards learning to manage the full range of emotions that make them (and us) human. The methods outlined here are designed to support young people and children so that they begin to have greater self-awareness, can develop an ability to know when it is appropriate to seek further guidance, and ultimately feel more in control of their lives.

The start

Our approach was developed over a four-year period with a group of 30 students, ranging in age from 11 to 16 attending a large state-run secondary school in the south of England. At its core we worked together to develop a value-based meditative and relaxation practice. However, as time went on, individual pupils who took part shared particular issues that also warranted our attention, and as a consequence we moved from focusing exclusively on meditative practice to also creating processes for exploring subjects as diverse as bullying, body image, positive relationships and how to feel more in control. What follows is a step-by-step guide for duplicating our practice of self-protection and emotional security.

Being student centred

Right from the start the project was student centred. I did not go in with a fixed sense of how things should be done; in fact, I was initially quite sceptical about the extent to which a meditative and emotion-focused practice could work in the busy setting of a large secondary school. The first thing I had to do was establish if anyone was interested in coming along to our sessions! I also wished to move away from working with young people on a one-to-one basis, and instead focus on working with young people as part of a group. From my perspective, one-to-one work would only serve to reinforce the narrative of adult as rescuer and child or young person as passive recipient of care. Instead, my intention was to treat young people with respect, and provide them with an opportunity to develop and shape each session alongside and in support of each other.

Group work

Over recent years, group work has gone out of fashion, and yet done well it can be an enriching and emancipatory experience. Supporting young people to come together as part of a group creates an opportunity for individuals to tap into the following values to:

- identify and share their own problems/possibilities;
- identify and share solutions/responses to life's challenges;
- take personal or collective action.

The overarching aim is for individuals to:

- feel less socially isolated and more able to communicate with their peers;
- develop stronger core-values and self-worth.

Opting in and out

Nobody was obliged to attend their group session; it was always an option to do so, and students could opt in and out depending on how they were feeling. This meant that some students opted out for extended periods and then opted back in a year or two later for a top-up session. The size and gendered mix of the groups also varied, and never went above seven students or down to less than three attendees. Some groups started as single-sex groups and only later, at the suggestion of students, went on to house a mix of boys and girls. Students were also aware that if a serious concern was raised it would need to be treated as a child protection issue and wider support might be needed.

Running the groups with the long-term aim of developing independent practice

There is no fixed way to use the approaches outlined in this chapter. It is possible to run core sessions over one six-week period, or you could choose to continue the methods that we developed for longer, perhaps over a number of years in the way that I did.

In our case, the groups started by meeting up once a week. Then, once the meditative and resilience-building methods were established, we moved to meeting once every two weeks, and finally to once every three weeks during the final two years of our time together. Whatever approach you choose, the singular objective is to introduce young people to a number of relaxation and meditative techniques with the intention that they will go on to practise both as part of a group and independently in their own time. Finally, because the sessions are designed for individuals to use in the long term, it can also be useful to extend the time gaps between each meeting. Doing so can create more opportunities for students to move towards independent practice under their own steam and learn the value of self-soothing when minor challenges occur in their lives. The singular objective is to encourage individuals to feel confident using the practices, in the hope that they see the worth in returning to them again and again across their life-course, and long after adult-led sessions have come to an end.

Self-referrals and general organisation

The student support co-ordinator initially referred young people to me if they were on a child protection plan or if they were regularly spending time in the school isolation unit. But as the months unfolded, word got out and students started inviting their friends along, and sometimes suggested that the group approach might be useful to a person who they thought was struggling with friendships or being bullied.

Over the course of each term, the meeting times were also switched around for each group so that the students' class times were not too badly affected. This meant that students could not just opt in to sessions simply to avoid one particular academic subject area! As the years went by, and students progressed up through the school years, they were invited to attend the sessions at break times rather than during class time, and most of them did so very happily.

Establishing ground rules and boundaries

From our first session onwards, we agreed on some ground rules, which included respecting each other's privacy and keeping any group discussions confidential. While the sessions were *not* a form of group counselling, it was likely that students would still sometimes share aspects of their private lives that they would not want to have more widely shared within the larger school community.

We also started each session with an invite for the group to decide what aspect of our practice to focus on. No matter how long students had been attending, it turned out that they always asked to start our sessions in the exact same way. At the time I was surprised but looking back I think the familiarity of the routine was grounding. Just as with younger children I have worked with, the secondary school age students preferred to establish a fixed routine within their meditative and relaxation practice, and seemed to find it reassuring to do so.

A starting point

It was on a cold crisp autumn morning that I pulled into the car park of the school that I would wind up visiting for the following three years. After introducing myself to the receptionist, I was greeted by a young pupil sitting at a student-run visitors' helpdesk who directed me down the empty corridor to the counsellor's room, a small and uninviting place littered with leaflets on safe sex and drug taking. A group of Year 7 students had already been allocated by their tutors to the half-hour sessions that I would be running that day. Among the students who would be joining me, some were recipients of pupil premium funding because they were in foster care or had been adopted, or because they had a social worker. Others were referred because they generally found being in school difficult, were socially isolated or were seen to be disruptive in class. Regardless of their background, the first challenge was to get a group of physically active and animated pupils settled enough to sit and focus in a way that might eventually lend itself to meditative practice.

Restless students need physical outlets

The first group that I met with was composed of five boys in their first year at the secondary school, who had all come from the same primary school and already knew each other very well. I could hear them long before I met them, and as they bundled noisily into the counselling room, I felt both anticipatory excitement and a feeling of being overwhelmed by the challenge that lay ahead. For the next five minutes they proceeded to talk over each other, shove, tease and ask loud and inquisitive questions. '*Why am I here, Miss, can I stay after this period so that I miss English?*' '*Do you like coming here?*' '*Are you a teacher?*' '*Do you have children?*' It was chaos. They needed to blow off steam.

For the first couple of weeks, they felt far more able to settle into sitting still together if we started our half-hour session outside in the fresh air, sometimes running around, gathering sticks and stones. Once they were tired, they lay down on the grass to look up at the sky and slowly counted backwards from 10 down to 1. Only after this burst of activity and restful contemplation did we go back inside to sit together in the counselling room, where I then gave each boy a hard-boiled sweet and asked each of them to see how long they could hold it in their mouth without chewing it (if you do this always check for dietary restrictions). This task not only required self-discipline, but patience and little talking. It also created space for the group members to be in each other's company in companionable and relative silence!

It takes time to build trust

It took about a month for the students to feel relaxed sitting alongside each other in my company. As Year 7s, they were coping with the huge adjustment of having transferred from small primary schools to the large secondary school where, because of its size, they were far less visible or known to the far larger population of teachers. Perhaps because of this they were keen to check in and speak during our meetings. Initially the boys in the Year 7 group would fall into the room, flop down onto chairs and talk over each other. We needed to come up with a way for everyone to be heard in equal measure. So, we came up with an idea, commonly used in group work, to place a stone we had found on one of our earlier outdoor phases in the middle of our sitting circle, and to use the stone as a guide to speaking. It was agreed that each person would have up to three minutes to talk and that they would do so only when holding the stone.

As time went by the boys became familiar with this technique and enjoyed taking part. They encouraged each other to actively listen in silence and to let the speaker with the stone, or shell, or stick, talk. Eventually, they also got into the practice of speaking to the experience of three positive events and three challenging events. But this end goal of containing and acknowledging difficulties, while also holding in mind some positive experiences, took some time to establish. At first, it seemed more important to get the boys used to talking in this way. At the time I was keenly aware that if I started directing their choice of subject area then I might lose them.

Online gaming, boyhood transition and toxic masculinity

When asked to talk about a positive aspect of their lives, young boys spoke predominantly about online gaming successes. The majority seemed to have free rein while at home to play online whenever they wanted, and sometimes long into the night. I was not particularly keen on discussing online gaming as an entrance into meditative practice, because on one level it was obviously counter-intuitive. On the other hand, I was also aware that online gaming really was central to their world and the subject provided them some common ground space to get used to talking to each other.

Our shift away from referring to online successes as one of the three positive aspects of their lives took place after a couple of months. It happened quite unexpectedly and organically in the aftermath of one of the boys speaking about his big brother having beaten him during a dispute over an Xbox handset. While Ollie was being commiserated with by the others in the group, he said, '*it's alright, it's just what my brother does, he's mad*'. His response was glib and very accepting of what sounded like incredibly aggressive behaviour, and so we waited and gave Ollie companionable space to sit with his feelings. After a few seconds, Ollie looked up and said, '*it's okay... it's what he does... he gets angry*'. And so, without any pre-planning, the subject of anger, provocation and justification for negative behaviours became central to our discussion!

What does anger look like?

I grabbed a board marker from the table, jumped up, drew a gingerbread outline of a person on the whiteboard with a line down the side and invited each boy to give a word for what they associated with acceptable forms of behaviour. Over the next ten minutes, the boys described older brothers and men as being physically strong, hard, tough and domineering. In essence they chose to describe a stereotypical alpha male. We then ran through their list of adjectives and I said, 'so it's okay for Ollie's brother to act as he does?' While most of the boys nodded and agreed that it was, one boy, Charlie, who normally took a back seat, quietly said that his stepdad never shouted, and that his mum had left his father because he had shown aggression and anger towards him.

Having listed all the behaviours relating to a tough alpha male, we then started to share how they felt around the type of man that they were describing, and quietly, one by one, they said things like 'he makes me feel scared' and 'I sometimes feel a bit worried'. Having run through the list of words to describe how an angry person makes them feel and said the words out loud, I asked each boy to think about the type of people they liked to be around. One by one they said that they would prefer being with people who did not get cross and whom they could be sure of. We ended the session thinking about how easy it is to lose our tempers and how much harder it might be to try to control a tendency to lash out, and then went on to think about different methods that we could use to keep our emotions in check.

The relevance of group work

Earlier in the book, we examined the trauma model and triggers. In this context it was important to keep discussions very general, and go with a pace led by members of the group. In this case, the boys had an intuitive grasp of when to keep silent and just let Ollie sit with his feelings. The empathy and concern in the room was palpable. If we had overtly focused on Ollie's situation, it might have been a trigger that led to him clamming up or feeling distressed. It had already been courageous for him to defy stereotypical expectations by confiding that his brother sometimes mistreated him. Opening up the discussion to everyone created an opportunity for other people to share their experiences on their terms and, most importantly, at their own pace.

At the time we came up with the following list of aims, which you and your group could add to.

1. Next time any of the boys got angry, they would reflect on what the triggers had been to see if they could pre-empt their behaviour when it happened again.

2. They decided that the stronger person walks away, thus dissipating the anger, and that taking long breaths and counting from one to ten might also help.

3. We also thought that we might try to visualise ourselves using an alternative approach and do so both in the moment and as part of a meditative practice (this last one was led by me).

A monumental shift becomes an opportunity

I also suggested that the next time we met we could move away from focusing on each other's successes online to instead focus our positive reflections during the first ten minutes of our time together on issues of real significance to them (from my perspective relating to emotional development). They could share any acts of kindness, and we would place a kindness tree in the corner of our room and record individual acts using tie-on labels (see Chapter 5).

In one case, a boy who said that he often lost his temper with his sister decided that he would try and do things differently and do something kind for her. Another older boy, Ben, decided that he would exit the room when his father shouted at him and would do everything in his power to not shout back.

In each case, I was struck by the pressures that the boys felt to adopt a very narrow definition of what it is to be an adult male. It was striking that once one boy spoke of his fear, the pressure was off and they all began to speak differently, with real pain in their voices, and with a level of openness that I could not have anticipated.

The experiences that they shared show how essential it is that we give all young children and teenagers the opportunity to talk and explore their feelings and associated behaviours with each other in a safe and supportive space. It also highlights that, given the space, they will come up with alternative narratives and share insights about the multiple and contradictory influences coming at them from wider society, social media and each other.

Girls, bullying and sexism

While some of the boys had been encouraged to join our sessions because they were reported to be acting out in class, the first group of girls that were encouraged to join my sessions had come to the group because they either were experiencing bullying, or they were managing difficulties in their home life and sometimes appeared anxious. Initially, five girls, in Years 7 and 8, were invited into the group. Of the five, three continued with our sessions for the four years that I was visiting the school; one girl moved on to a different school, and another girl stayed with the group for a year and then opted to leave.

As with the boys, it seemed that some of their difficulties stemmed from social pressures to behave in a certain way. For one girl in particular, Ella, break times were particularly difficult. As she walked the corridors, other girls in her year group would call her a 'slag' and a 'bitch', simply for being someone outside of their group who they did not like. While boys sometimes have to manage toxic forms of masculinity, there is evidence to suggest that girls also experience a feminine form of toxicity; consider, for example, some of the words used to name-call some of them. The terms '*bitch*' and '*slag*' are damning and cruel, and are purposely designed to make a girl feel very second rate.

As a group, we adopted the same opener that I used with other groups, starting by individually referring to three areas of strength and three areas that had been challenging.

During our first few weeks together, Ella was close to tears when talking about how other girls were treating her. She also made it clear that she did not want to talk to teachers about the specifics or let anyone know the identity of the girls so that their behaviour could be challenged. This lack of openness initially made the situation seem somewhat insurmountable. However, as Ella became more open about the way she was being treated, she also began to trust me and the other girls in the group enough to also speak about her own behaviour. As Ella walked around the school, she would react to name calling by responding using the exact same language as her aggressors. Sometimes she would also pre-empt their abuse by calling out the aggressors as soon as she saw them. As Ella spoke, my abiding sense was that the abuse would only stop if she changed how she interacted with the bullying group. So, I challenged Ella to do all that she could in her power to ignore the name calling just for one week; to find it in herself to simply walk on by and in so doing dissipate the other girls' hold over her by simply choosing not to react.

The next stage for all groups

Having established a trusting relationship within the group and a routine of opening each session with individuals sharing three positive and three challenging experiences, we then went on to develop the next phase of our practice, with the intention of working on feeling comfortable in the here and now and being in the moment. Both Ella, who was being bullied, but had inadvertently become sucked into also seeming like a bully by putting on an aggressive and protective front, and Oliver, who was being physically attacked by his brother, really needed to hold their own behaviour in check if any change was going to take place.

Stage 1 of meditative practice: becoming rooted and enjoying a feeling of being still

Years ago, when I was preparing for an interview, I came across a method to settle the mind and emotions which involved standing with feet apart and arms in the air, almost like a star. At the time, I tried it and it felt good. Having seen how much the boys had enjoyed being outside, I decided to have a go at mentally connecting and incorporating the wider environment into the star method, and thus the rooted tree was born!

The method is simple: instruct your students to stand with their legs slightly apart and to breathe slowly while imagining their breath flowing down through their bodies to the tip of their toes. If they feel comfortable closing their eyes they can do so, but this should be optional, for reasons outlined later in the chapter. Once the students are breathing slowly and regularly, encourage them to do so with their mouths shut, and breathe in through their nose for four breaths and out through their nose for six because this also slows down and regulates stress levels. As I also explained in Chapter 2, there is growing evidence to suggest that neurological development is affected by external stimuli. In his 1996 book, psychologist Daniel Goleman named emotional overreaction to stress 'amygdala hijack' (the amygdala being the region of the brain primarily associated with emotional processes). The amygdala hijack occurs when the amygdala responds to stress and disables the frontal lobes. That activates the fight-or-flight response and disables rational, reasoned responses. In other words, the amygdala 'hijacks' control of our brain and our responses.

Likewise, yogi practitioners have found that controlling our breathing creates a sense of control over our brains and emotions and calms down our thinking; once we can do this over a couple of seconds, the benefits begin to build. One simple practice to introduce is the simple 'through the nose, four breaths in and four breaths out', repeated a few times. I developed the tree rooting practice by asking students to stretch their bodies and imagine their toes sprouting like roots into the ground, as if they were a strong and grounded wise oak tree. As they rooted themselves, I suggested that they think of themselves as pulling energy up from the earth while thinking of themselves as strong, still and calm. At that point, we did some four breaths in and four breaths out breathing practice.

The first time I introduced this practice to the younger boys I found myself, in a Joyce Grenfell-like moment, gently reprimanding boys as they waved their 'arm branches' around and into the faces of each other! However, after a few hiccups, and relocating of 'trees', the approach had the effect of stilling most students across all the groups, including those who were generally considered to be quite hyperactive.

The appeal of this method is that it can be adopted with relative ease. After the girls and I had tried it out a few times, I suggested that Ella might go into the girls' toilets at the beginning of break and practise the exercises in the privacy of a cubicle to give her some strength of conviction before running the gauntlet of the corridor with a newfound grace and sense of being in control. The following week she reported back, and I could already see as she walked into the room that her demeanour was lighter. Using the approach had given her the strength to ignore her nemeses and to her delight they had quickly become bored with trying to provoke her; it seemed that their power was broken. I felt so proud of Ella. The outcome was beyond my expectations, and I was very impressed by Ella and her inner resolve and strength of personality to have stuck to ignoring the other girls. Meanwhile, as I will show later, among the boys some positive changes were also afoot.

Ethics around preparing to meditate or use mindfulness practice

Most of us would be hard pressed to sit still and centre ourselves with our eyes shut without doing some preparatory relaxation work. Some mindfulness practitioners introduce their sessions by inviting individuals to focus on a small object, such as a raisin. I thought it unlikely that this would work with the teenagers I was working with. Some of them would most likely eat the raisin or throw it at another member of the group. Instead, we needed something that was both engaging and a little bit out of the ordinary. So, I introduced the group to mood eggs, and gave each person one to hold in their hand and to look at as we went through our first stage of the meditative process.

To my delight and surprise, the mood eggs worked really well, and as I started my, admittedly off-the-cuff, relaxation script, I watched as individuals turned their attention from self-consciously looking out of the corner of their eyes at each other to watching with fascination as their mood egg slowly turned from one soft colour to the next.

While students looked at their mood egg, I also invited them to close their mouths and take three slow deep breaths in and five out. We then moved on to do an all-over body scan, starting with the feet and moving up through the body, inviting each body part to let go and relax.

Once we had relaxed the body, I then asked each person to imagine a golden light, like a shower of light drops running down over their bodies from the top of their heads and all around them, so that they could imagine the light forming a golden egg completely circling each of them. Once they felt encased in the light, I then asked them to visualise the light moving through and into every cell of their body and a feeling of being safe in that moment, saying *'right now, and here in this moment, with the golden light surrounding you, you are safe and nothing can harm you'*. We would then sit with this feeling, listening to soft music and focusing on the mood egg as it went through its colour cycles.

Being respectful and protective

One of the key outcomes of this practice has been to give children and young people some respite from the daily busyness and stresses of their lives. Some of the students I worked with were managing difficult school or home lives and at various times felt under threat. When I am training my social work students, we talk about the danger in assuming, without checking in, that a child's bedroom is a safe place for a child to be interviewed. Likewise, where a child has experienced abuse, they might also find an invite to close their eyes deeply threatening and triggering.

So, it felt really important to emphasise that during our time together they could relax and let down their guard. It was also important that each person was given space to figure out where they would choose to go to feel safe, so that their practice could continue undisturbed. For some, a safe place was their bedroom; others spoke of leaving their house and going to visit a friend or extended family member or visiting a secluded spot in a park, or even imagining themselves in a golden egg of light while sitting on the school bus.

The importance of remembering a happy moment or safe place

Early on in our practice we also spent a session thinking about whether individuals felt comfortable sharing an experience of a place and perhaps a moment in time when some of us had felt safe and content. The places of happy safety were varied. For one boy it was while hanging out and gardening with his mum; another person spoke fondly of cycling along the seafront of a nearby coastal town. Someone else said that being tucked up in bed was their safe place. Students were also interested in my safe and happy place, and so I spoke of the simple pleasure of simply sitting in a wooded glade with my partner.

The next stage

Over the coming months, we fell into a meditative routine of moving through the stages of individually checking in, to becoming a golden egg of light, and then, in our mind's eye, visualising ourselves floating out of the school building and up into the air, where we would feel the wind on our faces and the sun on our hair. As we floated away, I guided the visualisation by reminding students that, right there and then, they were safe and could, for that moment, create some distance from their everyday lives by looking down on the ground from up in the sky. Sometimes students fell asleep at this stage, and others wriggled and giggled. But over the coming weeks, the students always asked to go through the same stages again and again in the exact same way. Meanwhile, we were also adding new layers to the meditative practice and, without putting anyone under pressure, extending the amount of time that each person was able to sit still and relax.

Learning to fly!

Having imagined ourselves floating away, we sat with that feeling for a few minutes and then I guided the students to float down and into the place that was special to them (recall previous guidance on this point).

They could just sit in that moment and recall how the place made them feel, and as they did so we would root ourselves like trees in the ground, feeling the sun's warmth on our faces and wind in our hair. Students could root and feel the strength of the earth coming up through their toes, through the trunk of their bodies, and out into the branches of their hair and arms. All along we took slow breaths through our noses, three in, four out; five in, six out.

The overall response and observations

We had been meeting for a year and a half when I was unexpectedly called to the headteacher's office! By this stage the students were confidently using their own practice out of school, and we had moved to meeting once every three weeks. As far as I was concerned, everything was going quite well. I was both delighted and surprised by the pleasure that students got from our sessions, and I was also struck by each group's repeated request that we stick to the same routine and process week on week.

Having left an older boy, Ben, in charge, I arrived at the head's office where some parents and a social worker were introduced to me. At first glance I could see that the father looked quite angry and ready for a fight. The head quickly brought me up to speed. Ben's parents and the family social worker had come to the school for a meeting about how Ben was doing, and Ben's father was particularly upset by the work that he was doing with me.

I turned my attention to Ben's dad, introduced myself and told him how great his son was, and that I had just left Ben in sole charge of our relaxation group. He looked at me and with great agitation leaned in and said '*well, it's about that I have come to see you; what the **** are you doing to my son… and why are you putting him on medication!!*'

No doubt my face said it all. I quickly reassured Ben's father that I was not giving his son medication, but that we were taking part in guided meditation, which was a form of relaxing exercises that he and other students were developing together. Ben's father looked unconvinced, so I once again reiterated how mature and sensible Ben was, and asked him to talk a little bit more about how Ben was referencing his practice. He went on to explain that sometimes when he came home from work, Ben had taken to looking him up and down as he came through the door to measure him up and then decide whether to stay put or run up the stairs while shouting behind him '*That's it, I'm going up to my room to do Rachel's medication*'. I was also curious to find out more about how things might have been if Ben had not chosen to retreat to his bedroom. After a pause, Ben's dad shrugged and said '*well, if I have had a stressful day then we might have a bit of an argument*'.

I was secretly quite excited at this point, and also keen to reassure both of Ben's parents – firstly that they had misheard Ben and secondly that, overall, it sounded like a positive change was taking place in the family home! Finally, I said '*it seems to me that Ben is going upstairs to give you and him some space, so that you can both relax and avoid an argument … might that be a good thing?*' To my delight, Ben's dad agreed that it was making things better at home. As we closed the meeting, Ben's parents gave permission for Ben to carry on attending our sessions, and I reinforced how proud they must be of their son, who showed great kindness to the other students in our group. I also playfully suggested that he might also like to hear a bit more about Ben's developing practice and learn from his son!

As time went on, students would sometimes refer to examples of when they had used the practice outside of our sessions and some wanted me to do a recording that they could use on their phones.

Having established some support of the students in the here and now, it felt relevant to also encourage students to think about their life journey. After Ben's parents had visited the school, I felt even more determined to engage with students on another level. I had been struck by Ben's determination to break the familial mould and to behave differently to his father. I felt that that had taken real guts. So we did a little bit of life map work.

Life maps can be used as another prompt for supporting children and teenagers towards thinking about their future. This is an approach that social workers use in practice, and can be used in a variety of ways to reflect on key moments in a person's life and the aspects of their life that are meaningful to them.

In the past I have used this method and found it to be very useful, and quite helpful because it is so unthreatening. However, I have always felt that it could also be adapted to a person thinking about their future!

Looking to the future

The old adage that we do not choose our parents is key to this final stage in our meditative practice.

One of my motivators for writing this book is linked to the absolute vulnerability that comes with being a child or teenager dependent for their general well-being on parents and carers who might not always have their best interests at heart or have the capacity because of their childhood experiences to be consistently kind and helpful. As adults, we can forget that while we are growing up, our understanding of life is largely shaped by our immediate family, local community and school environment. Our experiences in each of those settings greatly influence our overall well-being and how valued we feel.

During a session three years into our meetings, a few of the girls opened up about feeling under pressure to have sex with their boyfriends. The school already engaged with the subject of safe sex, so instead of talking about the mechanics we started to talk about what the girls might be feeling, and began to share their long-term hopes for the future and for the rest of their lives. My rationale for taking this tactic was to support the girls so that they had space to figure out a bit about their sense of life purpose, and we looked at the poem 'The Road Not Taken' by Robert Frost. This led on, quite organically, to the group taking the meditative stages one step further. After arriving at our safe place and rooting ourselves, we then decided to visualise our life path rolling out in front of us, and move on from the life map to unfurl a future life!

Writing a piece about how we would like to be remembered

Our final stage was to jot down a few thoughts about what we would like to do with our lives and how we would like to be thought of by the people we love. Once each person had described a bit about their hopes, I encouraged them to simply think of their hopes as they visualised travelling their life path. While this might, on the face of it, seem a bit morbid, I have found the opposite to be true. The exercise became really popular with the students I was working with, and word got out. After speaking to their friends who had completed the exercise, other students would also ask to do so. The practice can be quite grounding because it takes us out of the here and now and any feelings of daily stress, and helps people look at the larger picture. When my eldest son was about 14 and feeling unexpectedly panicked about his future, I suggested he do likewise and he simply wrote '*I hope for a simple life, where I earn just enough not to worry, and I am loved and liked by my family*'. It was the loveliest of ambitions, and took him outside of the exam-focused panic to see that there was a bigger picture.

To sum up: once students arrive at the stage of being in the safe and special place and being grounded and rooted as a tree, they then move to standing, breathing in and then imagining themselves stepping out and onto their future life path. At this point I would generally say:

> *Look ahead and along your path, and as you slowly walk, putting one foot in front of the other, look around you, feel the ground under your feet and the sun in your hair; pay attention as well to the little paths taking you away from your own pathway... perhaps to a party you don't really want to go to, or into a relationship with someone who does not really know you. Whatever your path, it is yours, and right now, although you cannot control some of your life choices, you will be able to one day when you are older.*

Finally, some students also developed their own mantra.

Creating a mantra

I am cautious about the use of mantras, which are essentially words or phrases used to aid the meditative process. At their best they can aid and reinforce a personal goal or feeling. Some of the students I worked with found them useful when they were properly developed for their particular set of circumstances, for example when Ollie decided to keep his temper under control in the face of his brother's unkind treatment of him. On the other hand, they can also be quite glib. For example, saying something aspirational like '*I am happy and fulfilled*' can be counterproductive for people living in really challenging circumstances. There has been anecdotal evidence to suggest that we feel even worse after being advised to take up a life affirmation statement if we then do not have capacity to really embrace its intention. I think it is far more useful to embrace a manageable mantra, and ultimately to be kind to ourselves, no matter the outcome.

A final thought

Over the years of working in this way, I learned so much from each student. The desire to repeat the sessions and keep to the same script indicated a real need, among some, for stability and consistency. They were open, honest and kind, and worked hard alongside me to give feedback, guide me and develop our practice. By the time I left the school, most of the students had gone from being able to focus for five minutes to being able to sit for up to 25 minutes in a relaxed and meditative state. In practical terms, the time that we had put into each session was minimal and from the school's perspective time efficient: 30 minutes for each group once a week and reducing down to once every three weeks by the end of our time together. And yet, despite the infrequency of our final sessions together, students felt more able to manage their school life, and seemed to be better integrated and understood by other members of the school community. In short, the methods we used developed self-confidence.

References

Carroll, L (1865) *Alice's Adventures in Wonderland*. London: Macmillan.

Goleman, D (1996) *Emotional Intelligence: Why It Can Matter More Than IQ*. London: Bloomsbury.

7 Sharing our experiences with other professionals and academics

Do a little bit of good where you are.

Desmond Tutu

The more that our discussions about children and young people are dominated by an assumption that poor mental health is on the rise, the more likely we are to exacerbate and create problems where we could instead see opportunity for growth and change. I know, from talking to friends who are researchers, social workers, teachers, doctors and counsellors, that I am far from alone in wanting to move towards a focus on positive resilience building. In fact, there are already some fantastic pockets of very child-centred work taking place around the country. In some quarters of the medical profession there is growing concern about over-zealous use of medications. This is reflected in current National Institute for Health and Care Excellence (NICE) guidelines, which are now preferencing counselling over medication as a starting point for supporting children. The most recent report led by Professor Nav Kapur highlights value in preferencing counselling and mindfulness sessions over medication (NICE, 2021).

During the course of writing this book, I have had discussions with other professionals who, like myself, have an interest in working with young people but feel that they are doing so in a professional vacuum. For example, a couple of weeks ago during a visit to see my GP, we started talking about our work and the various points of common ground. She told me about a recent appointment with a teenager whose mother wanted him to go on anti-depressants because of his general low mood. On meeting the boy, she was taken aback to learn that his low mood was specifically related to the very recent death of a friend. The young boy was grieving and yet his mother had neither mentioned this to the GP nor recognised that her son's response was a normal reaction to a huge loss. In essence, he needed space to grieve and time to heal without feeling under pressure to do so. In this instance it would have also been helpful for the GP to know who to contact within the young person's wider community circle, a school tutor perhaps, or a specialist organisation in the third sector, so that he could benefit from wrap-around care via a number of avenues in his life.

Linking professionals up to schools

In 2012, the Munro Report (2011–12) recommended that professionals across different areas of expertise work together in support of children in their care. In some parts of the country this has resulted in local authorities linking a named social worker to schools in the area to enable more seamless support of children. Imagine if the GP mentioned previously had been able to contact the bereaved teenager's secondary school and be linked up with a school-associated social worker?

Programmes such as What Works for Children's Social Care (Westlake et al, 2020) receive Department of Education funding to place and monitor the outcome of placing social workers in education settings. Other innovative interventions include the talking to and listening to children (TLC) kit bags created for social workers to use in their communication with children, and which are supported by my colleague Professor Gillian Ruch at the University of Sussex (Ruch et al, 2020–21).

Creating personalised toolkits

One of my colleagues, Dr Kristi Hickle, is a social worker trauma specialist and leads support sessions and workshops on the subject. She encourages the women who take her classes to create their own comfort box or toolkit to dip into and use when they are feeling low or are triggered by past traumas. Personalised toolkits might include a music list, or a card instructing the owner to go for a walk, or a note to ring a particular friend; others might include a favourite photo, a cuddly toy or perhaps a mindful colouring kit. Whatever the contents, they are aimed at creating a tailored form of self-comfort and resilience and an individualised coping strategy.

A parallel with our approach

There are some parallels between this technique and the tailored visualisation that the children and I used as part of our meditative practice. You will recall that tailored visualisation involved individuals imagining themselves in a place which made them feel safe and content. Prior to incorporating this method into our visualisations, we took part in a group discussion on the subject. Some students shared both what their safe place was and, more importantly, the feelings that thinking about their safe place evoked in them. A description of each person's safe place or haven could be included in a personalised toolkit or comfort box, and the creation of a box could also be incorporated alongside other approaches outlined in this book.

Ideas for members of the medical profession

In the 1990s, some GPs in New Zealand started to give green prescriptions to patients who were presenting with low mood or with conditions that could be alleviated through regular exercise. Today, a growing number of GPs in the UK are also prescribing green and social prescriptions in recognition that getting outside into the open air, or being connected to a wider social support circle and doing some volunteering, can be restorative for people's mental and physical health (Robinson et al, 2020). Yet Robinson and his colleagues at Sheffield University found that GPs expressed some common but also distinct constraints to green prescribing, including a shortfall of funding and time, and a lack of awareness of the green prescribing concept. The constraint most frequently expressed by GPs was not funding but the perceived lack of available services (Robinson et al, 2020).

Yet the positive influence and respect for medical professionals should not be underestimated. It seems that green prescriptions become more effective when given out and prescribed on a prescription form that patients are expected to physically take away and act upon, and which they receive from a trusted professional in a familiar environment, such as from their GP or nurse practitioner at their health centre.

Although UK involvement in green prescriptions is still quite limited, this type of innovative practice is not new. In the 1990s, I worked as a social work student for the GP Dr Patrick Pietroni at the Marylebone Health Centre in London, where he used a similarly innovative approach with patients. His central aim was to expand the remit of the medical profession and to demonstrate the positive effects on patients of mainstreaming complementary therapy treatments within an NHS practice. The Marylebone Health Centre where I worked was established in 1984 and became recognised as both a national and international centre of excellence. Dr Pietroni went on to become the Dean of General Practice at the University of London and led UK Department of Health policy programmes, including Patient Choice, The Expert Patient and a Mentoring Support Group for National Health Service.

While working at the Marylebone Health Centre, I was struck by the way in which a more innovative approach could be introduced with no extra cost to the NHS. Dr Pietroni simply diverted some of his drugs' budget to the payment of sessions with complementary therapists whom he employed to work at his GP practice. They included an aromatherapist, acupuncturist, homeopath and myself as a counsellor/social work student. In his seminal book *The Greening of Medicine* (1990), Dr Pietroni argues that the bedrock on which modern medical practice is based is too science based, which results in little understanding of the 'whole' person and an over-reliance on hi-tech surgery and drugs. He suggests that the doctor/patient relationship should be more a partnership of equals, each with their own unique part to play in the process of healing. In the time I worked at his GP practice I was particularly struck by this aspect of his work, and it is an influence that has undoubtedly shaped my social work practice and approach to working with children. What follows is an example of the type of work I was doing while working at the Marylebone Health Centre.

In one case a woman, Jeannie, who had been asking for anti-depressants from Dr Pietroni, began to thrive and feel much happier once she had had three aromatherapy sessions with our aromatherapist and six counselling sessions with me, in which we worked out that much of her despondency stemmed from not having her own bank account and being reliant on her husband for money. Once Jeannie had access to the family bank account, she began to feel more upbeat and no longer asked for anti-depressants. By expanding our remit and thinking about the whole person, we were able to support some very real and meaningful change in patients' lives without any additional cost to the NHS. In Jeannie's case, the root of her depression was linked to feeling financially powerless in her marriage. Her husband did not want her to have access to the income that they earned from running their pub, and change would only take place if Jeannie felt able to develop the confidence to change the status quo. Her low mood was down to having little autonomy. If we had only followed her wishes and prescribed anti-depressants, then no real or meaningful change would have taken place.

Later, when I was qualified and working at Charing Cross Hospital, I continued to be influenced by the creative and person-centred approach that I had been so taken with while based at the Marylebone Health Centre. In one case I worked with a man whose depression and repeat admissions to hospital stemmed from feeling lonely post-retirement. During our chats I discovered that he had previously worked as a caretaker and really enjoyed doing DIY. A little while later, almost by serendipity, we visited a very cosy residential home, owned by a young woman who also lived on the premises and, like myself, supported innovative support. Within a month of moving in, Frank was happily finding new purpose to his life, going out to buy the daily papers for other residents and doing little bits of DIY work around the house. Moving to the residential home gave his life new meaning, mostly because the owner of the home treated him as an individual with a valued identity. It is vital to create innovative environments that give life meaning.

Likewise, the practices outlined in this book of setting up a kindness tree for younger children, and the three acts of kindness practice for older children also bring deeper meaning to their lives. Such practices can continue into higher education. At the University of Sussex, Professor Robin Banerjee in the School of Psychology has created a kindness project run by undergraduates, and also completed a number of studies looking at adolescent understanding of kindness and its links to well-being (Cotney and Banerjee, 2019). He and a colleague have found that showing kindness to others enhances personal well-being, but also that teenagers need to feel emotionally robust prior to taking part in altruistic practices such as thinking about other people.

Similarly, when working with my group of students, I found that the group environment enhanced each person's confidence in their ability to act kindly towards others, and that sharing purposeful acts of kindness also reinforced positive behaviour among and between members of the group. In some ways this highlights parallels with Cotney and Banerjee's (2019, p 613) study finding that adolescents also respond positively when given guidance on how to show empathy towards others. Moving away from thinking only about oneself can be challenging for anyone experiencing emotional challenges. Other ways of taking a person out of themselves involves complete immersion in the natural world, as is encouraged in Japan.

The healing benefits of being immersed in the natural world

In Japan, patients are prescribed 'forest bathing' or '*shinrin yoku*' and encouraged to walk among trees to awaken their senses and create well-being by immersing themselves in the natural world.

Likewise, when I first started working with some of the younger boys, I found that they became more relaxed when we chose to start our practice outside with a walking meditation. Our meditative practice of becoming rooted trees was purposely associated with the natural world. When we floated away and into our personally chosen place of safety, most of us landed up in an outside space somewhere in the natural world, and in a location that had particular personal meaning to each of us.

A walking meditation path

If a school or college has space for it in the school grounds, a walking meditation path can be created with and by students as part of a creative art or community project.

Creative school-based interventions

We can also do more to create innovative interventions for children and teenagers; recall the example of the headmaster at a grammar school who linked students to apprenticeship programmes. It would be really positive for children and their parents to be given green prescriptions from their GPs, nurses, health visitors, psychologists and psychiatrists to take part in a meditation via an app like Headspace, or to do some community-based voluntary work, such as a beach clean-up, or to take part in a Saturday park run. Approaches such as these link nicely to the higher realms of happiness associated with the positive psychology movement discussed in Chapter 4 and created by Martin Seligman. Embracing Seligman's ideas on deeper happiness linked to altruistic values can further help children and young people to feel happier, more motivated and less isolated. In essence, this philosophy of creating new meaning and motivation is behind my focus on group work for children and young people.

There are also numerous third sector projects that do something similar by supporting the development of a particular life skill, such as Ride High, which supports emotional well-being through caring for horses, and others such as The Wave Project, which supports the emotional well-being of young people across the UK by teaching them to surf and later asking students who have completed the programme to mentor younger people coming through it. In other words, there is real value in giving children and young people the opportunity to support each other.

Creating contemplative space

When I was working on the project for the Office of the Children's Commissioner England and visiting secondary schools around the country, I found that schools which reported high emotional well-being among students were also more likely to have created contemplative or safe spaces (Lefevre et al, 2013). Some of the schools also rejected the setting up of isolation units. Earlier in this book, I provided examples of poor practice in isolation units. It would be fantastic if schools at least experimented with switching isolation units over to emotional well-being centres that young people could go to when class or break time became overwhelming. Rather than have students sit and stare at a blank wall, they could be allowed in on condition that they did some schoolwork, or took part in a half-hour pre-recorded meditation, or supported other students with their studies via a peer-to-peer support programme, or perhaps took part in an out-of-school community project.

Like most of us, young people thrive when they are in creative environments in which the adults who support them practise boundary-based and respectful loving kindness, and most of them will also be aware of which adults in their life take pleasure from being punitive and finding fault. There can surely be no disputing that isolation units are punitive environments in which to place young people, and in my experience it is usually the same small cohort of students within any school that end up being sent into isolation on repeat. If acting out is a call for help, or a sign of past traumas, then is it now time to come up with more creative and humane interventions?

Final thoughts

My work has shown that we need space for contemplation in order to learn more about ourselves and to develop our resilience. Using the meditative methods in this book is useful for this and, as I show here, particularly in relation to the creative approach adopted by Dr Patrick Pietroni, practitioners do not need to be resource rich to instigate the ideas and practices that I have shared. In addition, there are already ample resources and funds directed at running isolation units in secondary schools. These could be re-organised and run as well-being centres without any additional costings in terms of staff time, particularly if the centres were peer-to-peer focused with older students mentoring younger ones.

References

Cotney, J and Banerjee, R (2019) Adolescents' Conceptualisation of Kindness and Its Links with Well-being: A Focus Group Study. *Journal of Social and Personal Relationships*, 36(2): 599–617.

Lefevre, M, Burr, R, Boddy J and Rosenthal R (2013) *Good Practice in Safeguarding and Child Protection in Secondary Schools*. London: Office of the Children's Commissioner.

Munro, E (2011–12) *The Munro Review of Child Protection: Final Report. A Child-Centred System*. London: Department for Education.

NICE (2021) NICE Creates New Menu of Treatment Options for Those Suffering from Depression. [online] Available at: www.nice.org.uk/news/nice-creates-new-menu-of-treatment-options-for-those-suffering-from-depression (accessed 18 June 2022).

Pietroni, P (1988) Alternative Medicine. *RSA Journal*, 136(5387): 791–801.

Pietroni, P (1990) *The Greening of Medicine*. London: Gollancz.

Ride High. [online] Available at: www.ridehigh.org (accessed 18 June 2022).

Robinson, J M, Jorgensen, A, Cameron, R and Brindley, P (2020) Let Nature Be Thy Medicine: A Socioecological Exploration of Green Prescribing in the UK. *International Journal of Environmental Research and Public Health*, 17(10): 3460.

Ruch, G et al (2020–21) The Kit Bag for Social Workers. [online] Available at: www.iffkitbag.com (accessed 18 June 2022).

The Wave Project. [online] Available at: www.waveproject.co.uk (accessed 18 June 2022).

Westlake, D et al (2020) *Social Workers in Schools: An Evaluation of Pilots in Three Local Authorities in England*. Cardiff: What Works for Children's Social Care, Cardiff University.

8 Concluding comments, exciting new possibilities and final suggestions

Inner peace begins the moment you choose not to allow another person or event to control your emotions.

Pema Chodron

When I started doing fieldwork for this book, I expected children and young people to be cautious about talking openly with each other about mental health issues, and resistant to practising restorative meditative relaxation techniques. I could not imagine any of the students I worked with using our methods independently and in their own time, and I also thought it unlikely that students would choose to meet with me over an extended period of time. I was wrong on all counts.

I learnt so much from the students during the five years of fieldwork. They taught me so much about childhood resilience and where that stems from, and about loyalty and love for family members. Some of them were insightful about the impact of being raised in challenging home environments. They were also keenly aware of how they were perceived by their teachers and the ways in which challenges outside of school were having an impact on their capacity to engage in the school setting. On the whole, they were open to using all of the techniques outlined in this book, and keen to share their ideas about which aspects of our developing programme worked and which did not.

Over time they blossomed in the group context, where they gained reassurance from listening to each other and learning that they were not alone in experiencing both the joys and challenges that life throws at us. Taking part in our sessions lessened their feeling of isolation and sharing acts of kindness developed their self-worth. The strength-based group approach that we adopted focused on acknowledging difficulties and the encouragement of mutual support in order to come up with new possibilities and ways to understand each person's circumstances. In essence, we used our sessions to give each person the opportunity to be heard, we developed relaxation and meditative approaches that could be used for self-healing, and we came up with new ways to understand their internal emotional landscape.

What fieldwork taught me

I have concluded from my work with children and young people that our contemporary treatment of mental health is fuelling an avoidable crisis. Contributing factors include a society-wide focus on the health of the individual out of context and a broader cultural shift towards lay people self-diagnosing mental health issues. We also have a society-wide tendency to both romanticise childhood and think of it as a time of innocence and lack of responsibility, while also playing down the pressures placed on children within our test-driven education system. In general, children and young people's perspectives are not properly heard or taken seriously, and because they are often treated as passive, it is perhaps no surprise that our tackling of mental health and well-being tends to be adult led and crisis focused.

As previously argued in Chapter 1, our societal approach to mental health is also one in which negative feelings such as sadness, anger and depression are increasingly treated as problematic rather than a manageable part of the human experience. There are marked similarities between my ideas and those of Dr Tracey Dennis-Tiwary, a US-based academic, who writes on the subject of anxiety. We both argue that societal ideas about mental health are culturally constructed, and in her case Dennis-Tiwary points out that experiences previously referred to as stressful are now more commonly referred to as anxiety based. Her findings indicate that we have an ever-increasing aversion to children and young people experiencing any type of negative feelings. She now refers to 'snow-plough parenting', a form of parenting in which adults will do anything to alleviate the slightest sign of unhappiness in children (Dennis-Tiwary, 2022). We both show that ignoring or suppressing negative emotions is more damaging in the long run and, like me, she argues that instead of trying to banish worries and feelings of stress or anxiety, it is useful for us to familiarise ourselves with why we began feeling those emotions in the first place. Only then can we address their root cause and then be supported to learn how to independently manage such feelings. It is this restorative approach to mental health that I have adopted, and which is central to this book.

Given the opportunity, children and young people are drawn to making positive change

You will recall that I was initially surprised by how enthusiastically the young people I worked with responded to our opening practice of sharing something positive and kind that they had done for someone else. The practice of sharing in this way also helped to highlight that we all have the power to choose how we respond to any situation. Our meditative practice of engaging and being rooted as trees supported a sense of each person being able to still and centre themselves, and we successfully used the analogy of our arms as tree branches waving in the wind to manage transitory feelings. No matter how challenging their circumstances, each student gained satisfaction from discussing a kind act with others in their group, and the simple act of sharing also further reinforced a positive sense of self.

A shift in our use of words

We were also able to think about all feelings and experiences as impermanent and began to move away from saying '*I have anxiety, I am depressed or I have mental health issues*', to '*at present I am experiencing this*'. In this way, we were reminding each other that our experiences do not define our identity or the way in which our futures will unfold. Instead, the practice we created supports a feeling of hopefulness that with sensitive support an experience will pass, and nothing is permanent. This shift in perspective also helps create a sense that change is possible, and links nicely to the practice of meditating the path of life, and a self-determined future, that the students in my groups enjoyed so much.

Early interventions as the best way forward

In the aftermath of Covid-19, there has been a greater commitment to providing mental health support services to young people. This is good news, but rather than provide reactive care I firmly believe that we need to focus on early intervention programmes aimed at entire groups of children and young people rather than one-on-one counselling support or support aimed at targeted groups, such as those who are already expressing unrest and unhappiness. The approach that I advocate normalises the importance of caring for one's emotional well-being, and creates a positive environment in which it becomes acceptable for everyone to talk more openly about their experiences, the emotions that they evoke and how to manage such feelings.

A focus on early intervention programmes also makes it easier and less stigmatising for children, teenagers and their carers to seek out more expert support if needed. The interventions outlined in this book can start the moment children go to nursery or primary school (see Chapter 5) and be slowly built upon as individuals go up through the school years. You will recall from Chapter 6 that the young people I worked with really valued the opportunity to talk about their feelings, and the space that our sessions created for each of them to learn more about how to manage the daily ups and downs of life. Pre-school, school or youth settings are good places for this cultural shift to take place, particularly because the time that the sessions take out of the average day is minimal. In all our school-based sessions, individuals felt listened to and their views and concerns were validated and addressed, but sessions such as ours could just as easily be run in youth and counselling settings.

It is also relevant to highlight that the type of group work I advocate is quite cost efficient because it is preventative by nature and places emphasis on children and young people individually continuing their practice long after the sessions have come to an end. Our focus on developing emotional resilience is key to hopefully avoiding later need for any form of costly crisis-led intervention.

We need to stop pathologising the normal range of human emotions

This brings me on to another important point. We need to change the way in which we talk to children and young people about their emotions and mental health.

First off, it would be helpful if we were to adopt a far wider range of words to describe how we are feeling. If everyone describes themselves using the same limited terminology, it makes it difficult to distinguish between individuals who are in real need and those who are experiencing a feeling that is more transitory.

Secondly, we need to let individuals properly express when they are upset or sad, and we need to give them space to sit with those feelings rather than jump in to reassure them, or immediately ask a medical practitioner to diagnose and medicate.

Thirdly, placing a child's experiences in the context in which they arise validates what they have been or are currently going through. A significant number of young people resort to using the internet and social media to create a self-diagnosis and to search out answers and explanations for any feelings of unrest, and they are most likely to do so when they are at a low ebb and by themselves. My students and I included discussions about the relevance and accuracy of online materials in our sessions. We also educated each other on how a diagnosis is made and which professionals are qualified to provide them.

Recall the experiences of Amber in Chapter 2, who was told that she was anxious by her social worker, but who had also shown courage and strength of character while supporting her mum and siblings (a fact that seemed to have passed her social worker by). Or of Ben in Chapter 4 who, using our visualisation and anger-management training, had successfully developed strategies to avoid confrontations with his father.

Amber felt far better at the end of our group session because we worked as a group to contextualise and properly acknowledge her experiences of sadness and loss, and also to validate and legitimise that it was understandable that she felt as she did. The umbrella term of anxiety, as applied by her social worker, in reality rendered the real Amber invisible and non-existent. Telling her she was anxious became the start and end point for the social worker; it was used against her and not as a starting point to also offer tailored emotional support and care, or to contextualise what was happening in her family and the caring role that Amber had been playing in being there for her mum. Instead of feeling worried about having a general label of anxiety that she was powerless to control, Amber left our session feeling okay with being sad about recent family events and with her self-worth restored. Quite right too! No one should tell a child that they are 'something' when they do not have the expertise to do so, and we should be mindful of the impact of our words and labels on the people we work with.

We should avoid stereotyping children and young people

While Amber was labelled as having anxiety, I found that individuals with neurodiversity were also sometimes treated in stereotypical ways by professionals. It is useful to give people a diagnosis, particularly for neurodiverse conditions such as autism, because understanding a condition can provide a positive starting point from which to support a person towards feeling more comfortable in themselves and with other people. But in some cases, a diagnosis can result in professionals only viewing a person through a limited and disabling lens. Recall how Jack's angry outbursts described in Chapter 4 were superficially and wrongly treated by teachers as simply down to an autistic tendency to lose control and become overwhelmed. Their assumptions about the source of his anger resulted in a no-questions-asked removal of him to the school isolation unit time and time again, without anyone trying find out the triggers for Jack being so upset.

Until Jack joined the meditation group, he had little means of expressing himself or any opportunity to gain trust in people and to recognise the value in being taught essential social and life skills. In this new, more nurturing environment, Jack defied some of his teachers' expectations of him. He thrived in the small group setting and enjoyed building friendships with some of the other boys in his group. It did not take the other boys long to see that there was a connection between when Jack 'kicked off' in school and when he had been treated badly at home, and they encouraged him to talk to his form-tutor. Building up trust within the group enhanced his capacity to communicate in a positive and reciprocal manner with others, and to feel part of the wider school community. As a result, Jack was no longer put in isolation when he got upset but was sent to the library to calm down, and he went on to become a year-group representative on the school council. In short, Jack valued the opportunity that the group gave him to develop social skills and spoke about wanting to have friends and to feel a part of a group. Another person with neurodiversity would have expressed their feelings differently. Children and young people with neurodiversity are as varied in personality and interests as any other members of the population.

We need to recognise that not everything has a quick fix

Some experiences cannot be quickly fixed, and it is important to acknowledge that this is the case. Some children and young people coming out of lockdown are struggling and we need to work closely with those who are feeling the impact, but we should not lose perspective. As I highlighted in Chapter 3, some young people who had been unhappy pre-pandemic thrived under lockdown. Life and our reaction to the challenges that we face are complicated by many factors. It is important to create opportunities for us to prepare children for the inevitable ups and downs of life rather than perpetuate the myth that childhood is a time of innocence, and that children and young people thrive best when growing up without responsibilities. In reality, having a complete lack of responsibilities during childhood is a phenomenon of privilege, which can be both infantilising and frustrating and render the adult powerful and the young person powerless. As I highlighted previously, some of the mental health issues that young people are experiencing could be attributed to a lack of opportunity for young people to act independently and grow in confidence as a consequence.

Physiological and restorative change is possible

In Chapter 2 I discussed the influence of the neuroscientist Sara Lazar's ideas on my work, and while I did not use MRI imaging to track alterations and recovery in the frontal lobes of the young people I worked with, I observed positive changes in their behaviour. Most of the young people who took part in my programme showed an increased capacity to manage and positively contain their emotions. They also came to our sessions happy to share weekly diaries, in which they had logged the time when they practised solo meditation and their motivations for doing so.

Finding joy in the ordinary

We would do better by our children and young people if we also embraced the positive psychology movement alongside mainstream psychology to show by example and deed that making a positive contribution to society leads to greater satisfaction no matter our personal circumstances. It seems apt to end with the words of Martin Seligman: '*Just as the good life is something beyond the pleasant life, the meaningful life is beyond the good life*' (Seligman, 2002, p 321). In short, all the children and young people we work with deserve to have a meaningful life; if they are to do so then we need to change our expectations of them and move away from any stereotypes that we might hold. It is important to work with them on the basis that they already have something to contribute to society and a desire to be properly heard. We should have faith in their capacity to actively engage with us.

Finally, we should place emphasis on introducing children and young people to supportive practices that they can also use in their own time in order to build resilience and learn more about themselves and their emerging identities. The goal should be to liberate the child's inner world, and to give each one of them faith in their capacity to grow and thrive without the ever-present need for adults to help them do so. That, of course, is the purpose of the approaches outlined in this book, which I hope you will enjoy putting into practice as much as I do.

References

Dennis-Tiwary, T (2022) *Future Tense: Why Anxiety is Good for You (Even Though it Feels Bad)*. New York: Little, Brown.

Seligman, M (2002) *Authentic Happiness: Using the New Positive Psychology to Realize Your Potential For Lasting Fulfillment*. New York: Atria Books.

Further reading

Alston, P (1991) *The Best Interests of the Child: Reconciling Culture and Human Rights*. Oxford: Clarenden Press.

Aries, P ([1960] 1973) *Centuries of Childhood*. London: Penguin.

Balagopalan, S (2014) *Inhabiting 'Childhood': Children, Labour and Schooling in Post-Colonial India*. London: Sage.

Bartlett, S and Burton, D (2010) *An Introduction to Education Studies*. London: Sage.

Berriman, L and Thomson, R (2014) Spectacles of Intimacy? Mapping the Moral Landscape of Teenage Social Media. *Journal of Youth Studies*, 18(5): 583–7.

Boddy, J, Statham, J, Danielsen, I, Geurts, E, Join-Lambert, H and Severine, E (2014) Beyond Contact? Policy Approaches to Work with Families of Looked After Children in Four European Countries. *Children and Society*, 28(2): 152–61.

Bourdillon, M and Boyden, J (2014) *Growing Up in Poverty: Findings from Young Lives*. London: Palgrave Macmillan.

Briggs, M and Hansen, A (2012) *Play-Based Learning in the Primary School*. London: Sage.

Bryman, A (2012) *Social Research Methods*. 4th ed. Oxford: Oxford University Press.

Burke Harris, N (2014) How Childhood Trauma Affects Health Across a Lifetime. TED Talk. [online] Available at: www.ted.com/talks/nadine_burke_harris_how_childhood_trauma_affects_health_across_a_lifetime?language=en (accessed 18 June 2022).

Burman, E (2008) *Deconstructing Developmental Psychology*. 2nd ed. London: Routledge.

Burman, E (2019) *Fanon, Education, Action: Child as Method*. London: Routledge.

Burr, R (2002) Global and Local Approaches to Children's Rights in Vietnam. *Childhood*, 9(1): 49–61.

Burr, R (2014) The Complexity of Morality: Being a 'Good Child' in Vietnam? *Journal of Moral Education*, 43(2): 156–68.

Burr, R (2015) Vietnam's Children's Experiences of Being Visually or Hearing-Impaired. *Disability and the Global South*, 2(2): 590–602.

Burr, R (2020) History of Street Children. In Cooke, D (ed) *The SAGE Encyclopaedia of Children and Childhood Studies*. London: Sage.

Burr, R, Shamser, S and Sutton, A (2014) Going the Extra Mile in Meeting the Needs and Expectations of Young Separated Asylum Seekers. In Cocker, C and Hafford-Letchfield, T (eds) *Rethinking Anti-Discriminatory and Anti-Oppressive Theories for Social Work Practice* (pp 60–77). Basingstoke: Palgrave Macmillan.

Cameron, C and Moss, P (2011) *Social Pedagogy and Working with Children and Young People: Where Care and Education Meet*. London: Jessica Kingsley Publishers.

Cathal, J and Widom, C (2014) Long-Term Effects of Child Abuse and Neglect on Emotion Processing in Adulthood. *Child Abuse and Neglect*, 38(8): 1369–81.

Clark, A (2020) *Listening to Young Children: A Guide to Understanding and Using the Mosaic Approach*. 3rd ed. London: Jessica Kingsley.

Cohen, L, Manion, L and Morrison, K (2007) *Research Methods in Education*. 6th ed. London: Routledge.

Coleman, J C (2011) *The Nature of Adolescence*. London: Routledge.

Cunningham, H (1995) *Children and Childhood in Western Society since 1500*. London; New York: Longman.

Donnelly, J (1989) *Universal Human Rights in Theory and Practice*. Ithaca, NY: Cornell University Press.

Dunne, M, Durrani, N, Crossouard, B and Fincham, K (2014) *Youth as Active Citizens Report: Youth Working Towards Their Rights to Education and Sexual Reproductive Health*. Project Report. The Netherlands; Sussex, UK: Oxfam Novib.

Esser, F, Baader, M and Hungerfood, B (2016) *Reconceptualising Agency and Childhood: New Perspectives in Childhood Studies*. London: Routledge.

Ferguson, L (2013) Not Merely Rights for Children but Children's Rights. The Theory Gap and the Assumption of the Importance of Children's Rights. *International Journal of Child's Rights*, 2(2): 50–81.

Freeman, M (2017) *Human Rights*. 3rd ed. Cambridge: Polity Press.

Fuller, T and Smart, T (2016) Working in Partnership with Adolescents in Care Who Have Experienced Early Trauma. In Richardson, M, Peacock, F, Brown, G, Fuller, T, Smart, T and Williams, J (eds) *Fostering Good Relationships: Partnership Work in Therapy with Looked After and Adopted Children* (pp 117–32). London: Karnac Books.

Gauvain, M and Cole, M (2009) *Readings on the Development of Children*. Duffield: Worth.

Gazeley, L, Marrable, T, Brown, C and Boddy, J (2013) *Annex A: Reducing Inequalities in School Exclusion: Learning from Good Practice*. Report for the Office of the Children's Commissioner for England. [online] Available at: www.childrenscommissioner.gov.uk/info/schoolexclusions (accessed 18 June 2022).

Gillibrand, R, Lam, V and O'Donnell, V (2011) *Developmental Psychology*. Harlow: Pearson Education.

Goble, C and Bye-Brookes, N (2016) *Health and Wellbeing for Young People*. London: Palgrave.

Hall, G S (1904) *Adolescence*. Stanford, CA: Stanford University Press.

Hampden-Thompson, G and Galindo, C (2015) Family Structure Instability and the Educational Persistence of Young People in England. *British Educational Research Journal*, 41(5): 749–66.

Hilder, S and Bettinson, V (2016) *Domestic Violence: Interdisciplinary Perspectives on Protection, Prevention and Intervention*. London: Palgrave Macmillan.

Hinton-Smith, T (ed) (2012) *Widening Participation in Higher Education: Casting the Net Wide?* Issues in Higher Education. London: Palgrave Macmillan.

James, A (2013) *Socialising Children*. Basingstoke: Palgrave Macmillan.

James, A and Prout, A (1990) *Constructing and Reconstructing Childhood: Contemporary Issues in the Sociological Study of Childhood*. London: Falmer Press.

James, A, Jenks, C and Prout, A (1998) *Theorising Childhood*. Cambridge: Polity Press.

John, M (2003) *Children's Rights and Power: Charging Up for a New Century*. London: Jessica Kingsley Publications.

Kassem, D, Mufti, E and Robinson, J (2006) *Education Studies: Issues and Critical Perspectives*. Milton Keynes: Open University Press.

Kehily, M (2015) *Introduction to Childhood Studies*. 3rd ed. Maidenhead: Open University Press.

Kennedy, S (2020) *Seeing the Child in Child Protection Social Work*. London: Bloomsbury.

Kerr, J (2013) *Judith Kerr's Creatures: A Celebration of the Life and Work of Judith Kerr*. London: HarperCollins.

Lefevre, M (2010) *Communicating with Children and Young People: Making a Difference*. Bristol: Policy Press.

Lewin, K M (2011) *Making Rights Realities: Researching Educational Access, Transitions and Equity*. Brighton: University of Sussex. [online] Available at: www.create-rpc.org/pdf_documents/Making-Rights-Realities-Keith-Lewin-September-2011.pdf (accessed 18 June 2022).

Littlechild, B and Smith, R (2013) *A Handbook for Inter-professional Practice in the Human Service: Learning to Work Together*. Abingdon: Routledge.

Masoumi, H, Roojien, M V and Sierpinski, G (2020) Children's Independent Mobility to School in Seven European Countries: A Multinomial Logit Model. *International Journal of Environmental Research and Public Health*, 17(23): 9149.

McCarthy, J, Hooper, C and Gillies, V (eds) (2014) *Family Troubles? Exploring Changes and Challenges in the Family Lives of Children and Young People*. Bristol: Policy Press.

McLaughlin, C (2008) Emotional Well-being and Its Relationship to Schools and Classrooms: A Critical Reflection. *British Journal of Guidance & Counselling*, 36(4): 353–66.

Montgomery, H, Burr, R and Woodhead, M (2003) Adversities and Resilience. In *Changing Childhoods: Local and Global* (pp 1–34). London: Wiley-Blackwell.

Morgan, D (2013) *Rethinking Family Practices*. London: Palgrave Macmillan.

NSPCC (2022) Keeping Children Safe. [online] Available at: www.nspcc.org.uk/keeping-children-safe (accessed 18 June 2022).

Oswell, D (2013) *The Agency of Children: From Family to Global Human Rights*. Cambridge: Cambridge University Press.

Panter-Brick, C and Feuntes, C (2010) *Health, Risk and Adversity*. Oxford: Berghahn Books.

Scheper-Hughes, N (1989) Child Survival: Anthropological Perspectives on the Treatment and Maltreatment of Children. *American Anthropologist*, 91(4): 221–3.

Seligman, M (2004) *Character Strength and Virtues*. Oxford: Oxford University Press.

Shepherd, J (2015) 'Interrupted Interviews': Listening to Young People with Autism in Transition to College. *The Warwick Research Journal*, 2(2): 249–62.

Sundhal, J (2017) The Political Space for Children? The Age Order and Children's Right to Participation. *Social Inclusion*, 5(3): 164–71.

Stephens, S (1995) *Children and the Politics of Culture*. Princeton, NJ: Princeton University Press.

Støro, J (2013) *Practical Social Pedagogy: Theories, Values and Tools for Working with Children and Young People*. Bristol: Policy Press.

Thomas, G and Loxley, A (2007) *Deconstructing Special Education and Constructing Inclusion*. Maidenhead: McGraw Hill.

Wells, K (2015) *Childhood in a Global Perspective*. Cambridge: Polity Press.

Williams, M (2020) *Children Who Change the World*. London: Walker Books.

Index

For Product Safety Concerns and Information please contact our EU
representative GPSR@taylorandfrancis.com
Taylor & Francis Verlag GmbH, Kaufingerstraße 24, 80331 München, Germany